Classroom Instruction From A to Z

How to Promote Student Learning

Barbara R. Blackburn

EYE ON EDUCATION

EYE ON EDUCATION
6 DEPOT WAY WEST, SUITE 106
LARCHMONT, NY 10538
(914) 833–0551
(914) 833–0761 fax
www.eyeoneducation.com

Library of Congress Cataloging-in-Publication Data

Blackburn, Barbara R., 1961-
Classroom instruction from A to Z / Barbara R. Blackburn.
p. cm.
ISBN 1-59667-038-X
1. Teaching. I. Title.
LB1025.3.B578 2007
371.102—dc22

2006102437

10 9 8 7 6 5 4

Editorial and production services provided by
Richard H. Adin Freelance Editorial Services
52 Oakwood Blvd., Poughkeepsie, NY 12603-4112
(845-471-3566)

Dedication

This book is dedicated to the kids in my life: Matthew, Jenna, Josh, Rebecca, Emma, and Asheland. May you all encounter teachers who help you soar to new heights.

Acknowledgements

To Mom, Dad, Becky, and Brenda—your ongoing support makes a difference in my life.

To my friends—your encouragement continues to fuel the fire.

To Missy Miles—your creativity is balanced by your editing skills—both of which made this book better.

To Lindsay Grant and Christy Matkovich—your research support was invaluable. Each of you inspires your students through your teaching.

To Bob Sickles of Eye On Education—once again, I am reminded of the value of a publisher who knows how to remove barriers to success.

To Frank Buck, Cynthia Kremer, and Don Stringfellow—thank you for your thoughtful feedback.

To my colleagues at Winthrop University—it is a pleasure to work in an environment that encourages productivity.

Finally, to the teachers in my life, my graduate students, those in Clarendon District One and in the Office of Literacy of the Chicago Public Schools, the individuals who shared their stories with me, and all those who have read my books and use the ideas to influence students—thank you. You make a difference every day in the lives of your students.

Meet the Author

Barbara R. Blackburn has taught early childhood, elementary, middle, and high school students and has served as an educational consultant for three publishing companies. She received her Ph.D. from the University of North Carolina at Greensboro. Now an Associate Professor, she received the 2006 award for Outstanding Junior Professor at Winthrop University, where she coordinates a graduate program for teachers, teaches graduate classes, supervises student teachers, and collaborates with area schools on special projects. She also regularly presents workshops for teachers and administrators in elementary, middle, and high schools.

She has extensive experience working with K-12 teachers providing staff development in the areas of school reform, instructional strategies, literacy across the curriculum, and working with at-risk students. Topics of her published articles include literacy strategies, high-performing schools, effective communication strategies, and grading/assessment. Barbara's workshops are lively, engaging, and filled with practical, relevant information.

If you are interested in contacting Barbara Blackburn, you can reach her at bcgroup@gmail.com or at her web site www.barbarablackburnonline.com.

Table of Contents

Acknowledgements v

Meet the Author vi

Introduction xiii

A Active Learning Is the Focus 1
- Attention 2
- Concentrated Effort 3
- Thinking 3
- Involvement 3
- Variety 3
- Engagement 4
- Active Involvement in Action 4
- Summary 5

B Background Knowledge Is the Foundation 7
- KWL Charts 9
- LINK Strategy 9
- Before, During, and After Reading 10
- Sticky Notes 10
- Picture Books 10
- Sharing What We Know 11
- Making Predictions 11
- Summary 11

C Choices Add Interest 13
- Tic-Tac-Toe 14
- Learning Centers 16
- A Final Idea to Start Off the School Year 17
- Summary 17

D Data: More Than Numbers 19
- Formal Data 19
- Informal Data 20
- Data About Your Lessons 21
- Using Data Effectively 21
- Multiple Sources of Data 22
- Making It Work 23
- Summary 23

E Expect the Best: High Expectations 25
- Expect the Best Through Your Words 26
- Expect the Best Through Your Actions 27

Belief . . . 27
Encouragement . . . 27
Support . . . 28
Time . . . 28
Expect the Best From One Another . . . 28
Summary . . . 29

F Focus on Your Purpose . . . 31
Where Are You Going? . . . 32
Where Are You Now? . . . 32
Why? . . . 33
What? . . . 33
How? . . . 33
Planning in Action: A Sample Map . . . 34
Summary . . . 35

G Graphic Organizers . . . 36
Weekly Vocabulary Study . . . 36
Graphic Organizers for Math Word Problems . . . 37
Comparing and Contrasting . . . 39
Summary . . . 40

H Help Me! . . . 42
Structured . . . 43
Understanding Is the Result . . . 44
Personalized . . . 45
Positive . . . 45
Options Within Lessons and Outside Class Time . . . 45
Repetitionless . . . 46
Timeliness . . . 46
Summary . . . 46

I I'm Listening…Or Am I? . . . 48
Guidelines for Listening . . . 49
Active Listening . . . 49
Fishbowl . . . 50
Morning Meetings That Spark Discussions . . . 50
Paideia Seminars . . . 50
Listening as the Foundation . . . 51
Summary . . . 51

J Just for Me . . . 53
Basics of Differentiation . . . 54
Differentiating With Text Materials . . . 54
Differentiating for Special Needs Students . . . 55
Using Homework for Differentiation . . . 55
Summary . . . 59

K Kick It Up: Adding Rigor to Your Classroom . . . 60
Ratchet Up the Complexity of the Task . . . 61

Increase Scaffolding. . . . 62
Guide Your Students 62
Offer Questions and Projects That Stimulate Open-Ended Thinking 63
Raise Expectations for Completion (Not Yet) 64
Summary. . . . 64

L Literacy for Everyone 67
Modeling. . . . 68
A Literate Environment 68
Comprehension Strategies 68
Writing to Demonstrate Understanding 70
Summary. . . . 72

M Making It Real 73
Relevant 74
Engaging. . . . 75
Application to Life 75
Summary. . . . 77

N Next Steps (Helping Students Break Down a Task). . . . 78
Start With the End 79
Chunking Content 79
Using Visuals 80
Skills Versus Processes 80
Support Without Creating Dependence 81
Summary. . . . 81

O Options for Successful Homework 83
Clear Purpose 84
Opportunity for Success 84
Focus on Quality 85
Extend, Reinforce, or Preview Content 85
Independent Work 85
Ownership 86
Feedback 86
Kid Friendly 86
Sample Homework Activities 86
Summary. . . . 87

P Perspective and Points of View 89
Comparing Viewpoints. . . . 89
Two-Voice Poems 90
Debates. . . . 91
RAFT Strategy 92
Changing Perspectives in Stories 93
Summary. . . . 94

Q Questioning Strategies 95
Quality 96
Understanding 96

Encourage Multiple Responses . . . 97
Spark New Questions . . . 97
Thought Provoking . . . 97
Individualized . . . 98
Ownership Shifted to Students . . . 99
Narrow and Broad . . . 100
Success Building . . . 101
Summary . . . 101

R Reflection Adds Depth to Learning . . . 103
Reflecting on What I Have Learned . . . 103
Reflecting on How I Learn . . . 104
Reflecting on My Progress . . . 106
Summary . . . 107

S Show Them What You Are Thinking . . . 109
Modeling Expected Instructional Behaviors . . . 110
Thinking Aloud . . . 110
Using Guide-O-Ramas . . . 113
Modeling a Process . . . 114
Modeling Instructional Expectations . . . 114
Summary . . . 115

T Turn the Tables: Helping Students Take Responsibility for Their Own Learning . . . 116
Responsibility Through Goal Setting . . . 117
Responsibility in Learning Activities . . . 118
Responsibility in Assessment . . . 118
Transitioning to Ownership . . . 119
Summary . . . 119

U Understand Your Audience . . . 121
Culture Boxes . . . 122
Venn Diagrams . . . 122
Creating Timelines . . . 123
Writing Autobiographies . . . 123
Writing Vision Letters . . . 123
Summary . . . 124

V Victory with Vocabulary . . . 126
Introducing New Words . . . 127
Checking Prior Knowledge . . . 128
Using Visuals to Enhance Understanding . . . 128
Playing Games . . . 129
Demonstrating Understanding of Terms . . . 130
Procedures When Encountering New Vocabulary . . . 131
Summary . . . 132

W Working Together Makes a Difference . . . 134
Structures for Effective Group Work . . . 135

Selection of Group Members 137
Roles for Group Members 137
Rules 138
Effective Groups in Action 139
Summary 140

X X Factor. 141
Clarify Your Vision 142
Hold High Expectations. 142
Operate from a Students-First Perspective 143
Inspire Your Students Through a Positive Environment 143
Count the Positives 144
Encourage and Motivate Yourself 144
Summary 145

Y Yawn! Reading Aloud Is Boring 146
Performing Without Practicing. 148
Other Options 149
Interactive Reading Guides. 149
Ensuring Understanding During Silent Reading. 151
Choosing Oral Reading 151
Summary 152

Z Zoom In and Zoom Out 154
Zooming In 155
Zooming Out. 155
Zooming In and Zooming Out 155
Summary 158

Bibliography. 159

Introduction

I believe in the power of teachers. But I have found that some teachers fall into the trap of looking for the latest "magic pill" to deal with the ever-increasing challenges we face in teaching today's students. The pressure to find an immediate solution to prove that our students are learning—according to a test score—outweighs our focus on long-term growth.

I am the daughter of a teacher and a school secretary. I taught in an elementary school and junior high school and taught beginning swimming to preschoolers and lifeguard training to high school and college students. Currently, I teach teachers in a graduate program at a university. I also worked for three educational publishing companies.

Those experiences taught me an important lesson. Teachers are *always* the key to effective instruction. It's not the textbook or the latest program on the market. In classrooms in which all students learn—regardless of gender, ethnicity, poverty level, or background—teachers do two things. First, they care about their students. The old saying is true. Students don't care how much you know until they know how much you care. But caring alone isn't enough. You also must connect with your students in ways that will help them learn. Throughout this book, the focus will be on foundational instructional strategies that will help you connect with your students. The best teachers use a set of core instructional strategies to positively influence the learning of their students. They don't jump from bandwagon to bandwagon; they do the things that work.

This book will not provide you with a lockstep program, nor does it offer a checklist. It is a set of recommended actions that, when persistently and consistently applied, will help your students learn more effectively. As you read, you'll find 26 chapters—one for each letter of the alphabet. The chapters are not sequential; rather, they are designed so that you can start with any area that interests you or that meets a current need.

Throughout the chapters, you will find stories about how teachers have helped their students succeed. In addition to reading about my own experiences, you'll meet teachers of all levels, from preschool to college, and teachers of various subject areas such as science, math, social studies, language arts, and music. The stories serve as lampposts, guiding you and your classroom in new directions.

You'll also hear the voices of students, whose names have been changed, in most instances, to protect their privacy. I love talking with students; they are, in many ways, our best teachers. If they believe you respect them and are truly listening to them, they will tell you anything you want to know.

It is my hope that you will connect with your students in new ways as you apply the strategies in the following chapters. But I also hope that you will feel a sense of renewal. As I travel across the nation, I am saddened as I listen to teachers share their feelings of discouragement. As you read, you'll find a common thread throughout every chapter. Teachers do make a difference in the lives of their students. Despite what you may feel, in spite of the negativity that can drag you down, never forget that you are important. You make a difference for your students, and you can positively influence them in exciting ways as you try the strategies suggested here. Learning is an adventure—enjoy the journey!

FYI

Electronic versions of selected figures from this book are available at http://www.barbarablackburnonline.com

A

Active Learning Is the Focus

Tell me, and I forget. Show me, and I may not remember. Involve me, and I understand.

Native American saying

One of the hottest topics in education today is active learning. A recent Google search, for example, returned more than 84 million hits, so it is definitely a popular subject! What does active learning really mean? Most definitions include words such as *activity*, *engagement*, and *involvement*. Here's my simple explanation: Active learning is like a Slinky. Have you ever played with a Slinky? Even as an adult, it is one of my favorite toys. It's hard to be stressed out when you have one in your hands.

But the key to the Slinky is this: You have to use two hands to make it go back and forth. If you hold it in one hand, it just sits there, doing nothing. It doesn't move correctly without both ends working. Likewise, if the teacher is the only one involved in the lesson, it isn't effective. Both the teacher and the student must be involved.

Think About It

How involved are your students in their learning? Are they holding up their end?

The foundation of active learning is involvement by both the teacher and the student. I recently spoke with a teacher who wanted me to give her a list of active versus passive learning strategies. But it's not that simple. For example, if a teacher lectures, is that a passive activity? Not necessarily. I've been on the receiving end of lectures that were very engaging; I was totally involved, taking notes and making connections to my prior experiences and my current situation. When I was in college, though, I remember a professor who lectured throughout the entire course. I wrote on notepaper during class, so he thought that I was focused on his class. In reality, I was working on my homework from another course! It isn't the strategy—it's how you use the strategy that makes a difference.

Students who are actively involved in a lesson or activity exhibit several key characteristics:

ACTIVE

A	Attention
C	Concentrated effort
T	Thinking
I	Involvement
V	Variety
E	Engagement

Attention

When a student is actively engaged in your lesson, he or she pays attention. That may sound simple, but it isn't. Some students look at the teacher, but their minds are actually a million miles away. Paying attention means that students are actually focusing on what is going on in the classroom. It's important to craft lessons that require students to pay attention to the task at hand. In every lesson or activity, you should provide an opportunity for students to do something. Ask them to create an example, build a model, draw a picture, write notes, or stand up and demonstrate what they have learned.

Concentrated Effort

Students are more likely to be engaged when the lesson isn't too easy, when it requires some effort on their part. I'm skilled at multitasking, and in today's society, we wear that as a badge of honor. But when I'm working on something important or learning something new, I focus completely on that one thing. In order to involve students, create activities that demand they concentrate solely on the task at hand and put forth effort.

Thinking

When students are actively involved in a lesson, their brains are spinning. They are thinking about what has just happened, how it connects to something they already know, and how they might use the information later. In each lesson, how do you give students opportunities to think?

Involvement

As I said earlier, involvement is the foundation of active learning. Sometimes, involvement can be physical—such as, when a student builds a model of a roller coaster to demonstrate the principles of physics. But involvement is also mental, taking place when students make the connections I just described. It's difficult to gauge when a student is actually involved, so don't jump to conclusions. A teacher in one of my workshops spoke to me at a break. She said, "I don't want you to think I'm not paying attention. I know you probably saw me drawing, but I'm an art teacher, and the best way for me to process is through pictures. So I've been drawing out visuals of all your ideas." Watch your students, talk to them, and be open to different ways of being involved.

Variety

One way to ensure active involvement is to vary the activities in your classroom. Even the best, most interested students can become bored. For example, Jason Womack, a former middle and high school teacher in Ojai, California, designs his 50-minute class blocks to include a variety of activities. He organizes his instruction around a theme for the day and always lists 5 to 12 activities on the board. He wants his students to see, hear, and touch something at least twice every day. In a typical day, Jason's students will "see something, hear about it, and produce something based on what they heard (e.g., draw, write, make a video, or create a puppet show). My goal is to give them information and let them internalize and give it back; not just force-feed info and make them regurgitate it. I want to give them an opportunity to internalize and express [their learning]."

Engagement

The final component to active involvement is engagement. Are your students actually engaged in the activity? In my book *Classroom Motivation From A to Z,* I discussed ways to increase student engagement based on lessons that I learned watching kindergarten teachers.

All I Ever Needed to Know About Student Engagement, I Learned Watching Kindergarten Teachers

Make it fun, and learning happens.
Build routines, and everyone knows what to expect.
Keep students involved, and they stay out of trouble.
Make it real, and students are interested.
Work together, and everyone accomplishes more.

When you intentionally apply these principles, your students will be more engaged in learning and will achieve at higher levels.

Active Involvement in Action

What does a lesson look like when students are actively involved? Scott Bauserman, a teacher at Decatur Central High School in Indiana, asks his students to choose a topic from the social studies unit and design a game. The finished product must teach about the topic, use appropriate vocabulary and processes, and be fun to play. As he explains, "Students have to construct the game, the box, provide pieces and a board, and write the rules. I received a wide variety. One game I will always remember was about how a bill gets passed into law. We spent time [in class] talking about all the points where a bill in Congress or the state General Assembly could be killed, pigeon-holed, or defeated. The student took a box the size of a cereal box, set up a pathway with appropriate steps along the way, constructed question/answer cards, and found an array of tokens for game pieces. If a player answered a question correctly, he or she would roll a dice and move along the path to passage. But the student had cut trap doors at the points where a bill could be killed, and if a player landed on a trap door/bill stopper, the player to the right could pull a string, making that player's token disappear from the board. The player would have to start over. Not a bad game from a student who has fetal alcohol syndrome and is still struggling to pass his classes."

A favorite activity in my workshops comes from Kathy Bumgardner, a former reading specialist for the Gaston County Schools. *Be the Sentence* is a way to help students understand the basic principles of grammar. You might think that grammar is boring, a topic that's impossible to teach in a way that actively involves students. That's exactly why I use this activity: It shows teachers that anything can be engaging. In the activity, students actually become the sentence. Each student receives a card with a word or punctuation mark on it, and together, they act out the sentence, creating the emotion that is appropriate to the punctuation mark.

Imagine learning grammar this way. Students actually see the importance of punctuation and the effect that punctuation has on the tone of the sentence. Too often, students think that punctuation is just something to put at the end because the teacher said so. The demonstration, along with the student interaction, creates a memory as to the true purpose of grammar. And that is the ultimate purpose of active learning—to learn!

Summary

- Active learning requires both the teacher and the student to have an integral role in the acquisition of new knowledge and skills.
- The key components of active learning are attention, concentrated effort, thinking, involvement, variety, and engagement.
- Learn is an action verb. Get your students up and moving whenever possible.

If You Would Like More Information…

Active Learning: 101 Strategies to Teach Any Subject by Mel Silberman, Allyn and Bacon.

Applying Standards-Based Constructivism: A Two Step Guide for Motivating Middle and High School Students by Flynn, Mesibov, Vermette, and Smith, Eye On Education.

Fresh & Fun: Teaching with Kids' Names*: Dozens of Instant and Irresistible Ideas and Activities That Build Early Literacy,*

Math Skills, and More from Teachers Across the Country by Bob Krech Scholastic.

Algebra Out Loud: Learning Mathematics Through Reading and Writing Activities by Pat Mower, Jossey-Bass.

Teaching Out of the Box: A Teacher's Guide to Making History Fun…and More! By Stan Cody, Stan Cody Publishing.

Teaching Literacy Through Drama: Creative Approaches by P. Baldwin, Patrice Baldwin, & Kate Fleming, Routledge Falmer.

Directions Connections by Dorothy VanderJagt, Incentive Publications.

Classroom Motivation from A to Z, by Barbara R. Blackburn, Eye On Education. (See chapter E).

B

Background Knowledge Is the Foundation

A little knowledge is a dangerous thing, but it sure beats a blank stare for starting a conversation.

Anonymous

One of the keys to helping students learn is to make sure they build a strong base for new information. Last summer, my friend's son built a stone garden in my yard. First, he put down a layer of stone, checked to see that it was level, and then added sand and gravel to make the ground under the stone was even so that the first row would completely level. It took him much longer to do the bottom row than the top three rows. He explained to me that if the foundation isn't right, the entire garden wall would be flawed. This is also true with learning.

For our students, the foundation is the knowledge they already have about a topic. To effectively teach students something new, we need to know what they already know or think they know about a particular concept. In some instances, they have knowledge that is incorrect, and we need to address their misconceptions in a way that leads them to understand the concept correctly.

For example, I was observing Mandy, a student teacher in a kindergarten classroom. As she began to read to the class, she introduced the book by saying, "Today, we're going to read a book about farms." As she read, the students continued to raise their hands, saying, "That's not what's on a farm." After the lesson, she realized she had forgotten to find out what they already knew before she started. The book depicted what many would consider a typical farm, with cows, chickens, a tractor, and a farmer. But she was teaching in an area where tobacco farming was the norm. I explained that farming is one of those concepts that we think is simple, but it is actually complex. Just in North and South Carolina alone, there are tobacco farms, turkey farms, peach farms, and Christmas tree farms. If she had started the lesson by asking her students to describe things that are found on a farm, she would have been able to use that information to help her students compare different types of farms, and her students could have connected their prior knowledge to the new story.

It's critical to understand your students' prior knowledge. If teaching is helping students move from where they are to where they need to be, you must know where they are. We'll talk more about this is Chapter U, "Understand Your Audience," but here we want to focus on understanding what your students currently know (or think they know) in order to help them connect with the new information you are teaching. Don't skip this part. Your success at helping your students connect what they already know to the new content will determine how well they will retain the new knowledge. We'll look at six strategies for understanding and building background knowledge:

Strategies

KWL charts
LINK strategy
Before, during, and after reading
Sticky notes
Picture books
Sharing what we know
Making predictions

KWL Charts

Probably the most common method of identifying students' prior knowledge that I see in classrooms today is a KWL chart. During a KWL activity, you ask the students what they already know about a topic (K) or what they think they know about it. Next, you ask what they want to know (W). Then, you teach the lesson and ask them what they learned (L).

LINK Strategy

Kendra Alston adapts the KWL strategy into a LINK for her students.

L	I	N	K
List everything you know	Inquire about what you want to know	Now we are going to take notes	What do you now know?

After they complete the L column individually, her students turn to a partner and share their answers. Then, she leads a short class discussion, charting out what everyone in the class knows about the topic. As she works through the lesson, students finish by writing what they now know (K), and they tear that part off to turn in as they leave her class. This provides her immediate feedback as to what her students learned or didn't learn in class.

It's important to share students' responses with everyone, albeit it in a safe way that doesn't embarrass anyone. That's why I like her method. She starts by allowing each student to write an individual response, so everyone has an opportunity to think about what they know. As Kendra points out, if I'm a student, "by sharing with a partner, I can feel 'safer' in case I'm not right. In the whole class discussion, I'm sharing 'our' answers (mine and my partner's), so I don't feel like I'm out on a limb by myself. You could even add another option of sharing with two groups of partners before you share with everyone. However, don't sacrifice the whole class discussion. We all learn more together, and it's a safe guess that someone in my class knows something I don't know. Listening to all responses and charting them out for everyone to see helps me build prior knowledge when I don't have much."

Before, During, and After Reading

Another variation is to have students use a bookmark as they read. The bookmark is divided into three sections: Before, During, and After. Before they read, students jot down what they know or think they know about the subject. As they read, they make notes about the text. You can choose to focus their reading—for example, by asking them to list the main idea of each section or describe the causes and effects of an event. After the students finish, they write one or two things they want to know or want to learn more about.

Sticky Notes

Missy Miles describes an alternative approach to assessing background knowledge: "As students come into class I hand each of them their own sticky note (which they love). I have a question or other directions written on the board that ask the students to tell me what they know about the topic we are beginning that day in class. For example,

'List five things you already know about William Shakespeare' or 'What do you know about the Holocaust?' The students respond to the statement or question on their sticky notes and then place their notes on the board. After all students have responded, I read each of the sticky notes out loud, often times categorizing their responses into appropriate fields. By verbally acknowledging each sticky note, all students feel as though they have contributed to the 'background knowledge board.' More importantly, many students realize they know more about the topic than they first thought as they recognize other students' responses. I hear whispers in the class such as 'Oh, yeah,' or 'I knew that!" It causes students to feel as though they can be successful at learning this subject because they already know something about it."

Picture Books

When I was teaching, I used picture books to help students build background knowledge. Because I planned to teach in the primary grades, I had a large collection of books. When I was teaching older students, I found that picture books were a safe way to introduce information to them. I explained that our task was to evaluate how "good" the book was, so we read it before our lesson, then revisited it after the lesson to determine whether the author was correct. My students loved catching an author in a factual error, and it allowed me to help them build a base of knowledge before the lesson.

Sharing What We Know

At times, Missy asks her students to work in small groups to write facts about a particular topic. As a sheet of paper comes around, students write one thing they already know and then pass it to their neighbor. The paper continues around the circle. When it comes around a second time, students can add an additional fact, making sure not to repeat anything that another group member has already stated. This continues until the group has exhausted all thoughts on the subject. Next, switch papers among the groups and ask them to read the other group's list and see whether there's anything they can add to it. As Missy explained, "More than likely, they'll see something on the other group's list they hadn't thought of or didn't know."

Making Predictions

A final way to help students think about what they already know is by asking them to make predictions. Before they read a story or before you begin your instruction on a particular topic, give them a list of vocabulary words. Ask students to work in groups to circle the words they think relate to the upcoming lesson, draw a line through the ones they think won't be related, and put a question mark beside ones they don't know. After the lesson, the students return to the lists to see which ones they predicted correctly. Having a set of words to jump-start the discussion prompts them to think of ideas that would not have emerged with the open-ended activities, such as a KWL.

In each of these activities, the purpose is not that students are correct in their answers. You want to learn their true knowledge base as well as their misconceptions so that you can address those issues in your instruction. Your best teaching comes when you start where your students actually are, not where you think they are.

Summary

- Background knowledge is the foundation a student's learning process. Make sure it's solid and firm.
- We must find out where students are before we can walk them to a new place of understanding.
- The rate at which you help students retain new information depends on how well you connect it to what they already know.

- There are many ways we can tap into a student's prior knowledge. Whichever method you choose, be sure it gives you an accurate, thorough idea of what your students know.

If You Would Like More Information...

This site contains an article that discusses the importance and the effectiveness of activating background knowledge. http://www.cast.org/publications/ncac/ncac_backknowledgeudl.html

This site contains a lesson plan about activating background knowledge. http://www.nclrc.org/materials/lessons/lslesson1.html

Building Background Knowledge for Academic Achievement: Research on What Work in Schools by Robert J. Marzano, Association for Supervision and Curriculum Development.

C

Choices Add Interest

It is our choices, Harry, that show what we truly are, far more than our abilities.

J. K. Rowling
author of the *Harry Potter* series

Offering choices is one of the simplest ways to encourage student involvement in your classroom. Unfortunately, I talk to many students who feel as though they never have any choices. I spoke with one student who told me he felt that school is a place where "they tell you what to do all the time." Feeling a lack of choice is disheartening and frustrating for anyone.

There are many opportunities for students to have choices in your classroom. It's fairly easy to give students choices; it just takes a little extra planning. You can allow students to choose what they read, how they respond to the reading, how they learn, or what topics they research. One of the most basic ways to give students a choice is to allow them to choose how they will demonstrate their understanding of the content. When I assigned a book report, for example, my students could choose the desired format. Imagine the depth of understanding needed for a student to summarize a book in a two-minute commercial or the creativity involved in developing a music video to explain the content. If they are allowed to choose how they will show that they understand the content, many students will invest more time and effort in the task.

Lindsay Grant, a high school math teacher, takes this idea to a higher level by allowing her students to choose the problems to solve on an assessment. "I might have them choose two out of the five problems listed. This seems to relieve some of the stress from taking a test."

Marcia Alexander, an English teacher at West Mecklenburg High School, allows her students to choose a writing topic. "I give students the choice to choose their topic because if they are interested in what they are discussing, they tend to elaborate more effectively, as opposed to when I choose the topic for them. When students are given the opportunity to choose their topic, they are more willing to perform the task and usually do a better job. After modeling effective strategies and discussing the purpose and audience for a persuasive piece, I will list several prompts in the form of should/should not or agree/disagree and ask students to choose the prompt they're most interested in writing about."

In each of these examples, the teacher balanced choice with structure. Rather than saying, "Choose whatever you would like to do," each teacher said, "Choose from these options." That's appropriate, and it reflects the adult world. In most situations, you are asked to choose among several options, whether it is the purchase of a car or a job offer. When I work with graduate students, I tend to allow more flexibility in their options, but even then, I have structure. If a graduate student wants to pursue a topic for a project and it isn't one that I've recommended, I think, "Does it count?" using a set of guidelines.

Does It COUNT?

C	Connected to our topic
O	On an appropriate level (not too easy, not too hard)
U	Understandable to you as the teacher
N	Not a repeat of earlier work
T	Thought provoking

Now that you have a foundation of ideas that provide choices for students, let's look at specific examples of games and activities that incorporate choice. Each can be adapted for use with any subject you teach.

Tic-Tac-Toe

Diane Owens, a math and science teacher, uses a Tic-Tac-Toe handout with nine different assignments. She varies the activities, and students choose three assignments of greatest interest.

Tic-Tac-Toe

Interview three people outside Grandview to discover how math is used in their jobs. Develop a set of five questions to be used during the interview, and leave a space for the signature of the person being interviewed. Present the questionnaire for teacher approval before beginning the interviews. If possible, obtain copies of graphs, charts, and forms to illustrate. After the interviews, write a summary paragraph of at least five sentences. Put all of the information into booklet with each interview and paragraph on a separate page. Present it to the class.	Mystery packet of career/consumer math problems.	Collect two examples of each of the following types of graphs: bar, circle, line, and pictograph. (Cannot be from a math textbook.) Organize the graphs into a booklet, with one graph per page and a paragraph of at least five sentences discussing the type of graph, the information presented in the graph, the usefulness of the graph, and who would use the information in the graph and why.
Construct a calendar page for any month except February. For each day, create a math problem whose answer is the date that it represents, its opposite, its reciprocal, or its negative reciprocal. Use as many different types of problems as possible, but create at least 10.	Design a crossword puzzle using vocabulary terms from the current chapter of study.	Each day, record the number of gold, silver, and bronze medals won by the U.S. Olympic team and then create a graph to display the information. Make the poster as attractive as possible.
Find at least five advertisements on television, in the newspaper, or in a magazine that use misleading statistics Describe (television) or cut out the advertisement and explain why the statistic is misleading. Display the information as a booklet or poster.	Research and obtain two data sets regarding the Olympics and compare using box and whisker plots. Display both plots on a poster board or on large construction paper. Examples of data sets are the number of medals awarded to countries in Europe compared to Middle Eastern countries. Or, include a breakdown of medals won in each event for two countries, such as the United States and Canada.	In your math book, complete page 128 (Discovering Algebra). Display the data on a poster, making it as attractive as possible.

You must choose any three assignments in Tic-Tac-Toe fashion and complete one assignment each week for the next three weeks. The first assignment is due on February 17, the second is due on February 24, and the last assignment is due on March 3. These will be your problems for the next three weeks, so choose wisely.

I understand that I am to complete one project each week for the next three weeks.

Signature: ____________________ Date: ____________

Learning Centers

Learning centers are popular in primary classrooms, but they are appropriate at all levels. In addition to providing choices for students, the independent nature of the work helps them take responsibility for their own learning, which we'll discuss in Chapter T, "Turn the Tables."

Lori Osburn uses learning centers not only to teach content but also to help her students learn to work independently at a young age. "I had center time in my classroom every day. My students had 10 centers to rotate through each week. They were completely responsible for choosing which center to go to and for rotating through them all. As they completed a center, I checked their work and checked them off on their personal check sheet that they kept in their desk. When all centers were completed they were called "superworkers" and received a paper badge to wear home on Friday with the theme of the week. The kids loved this time to work independently. They didn't realize they were doing 'work' and learning, they just thought they had free time to complete activities in the classroom. Center time also served as a valuable lesson in time-management that definitely had to be learned, especially with the young ones."

With older students, you might structure the activities differently. Christy Matkovich, a math teacher, uses learning centers to enhance the small-group activities she utilizes in her classroom. "At each center there are four different folders, with a number (one through four). When it is center time, if a child sits at a one in his or her group, then he or she may choose a center and complete the activity in folder number one at that center. If a child sits at the three spot in his or her group, then during center time, he or she may choose a center and complete the activity in the folder number three at that center. When preparing activities for each center, I make sure that the concept for all four folders is the same. For example, at center number one, everyone may be working on concepts that involve order of operations. However, the level of difficulty varies based on the folder number. Folders one and two are basic activities, and folders three and four are enrichment activities. This arrangement allows me to challenge the higher level students and do some remediation for the lower level students. Some centers are set up so that ones and fours work together and twos and threes work together. Although my ones and twos are low, I still want to challenge them. Therefore, on challenging activities, I pair them with the higher-performing students so that they can help and support each other."

A Final Idea to Start Off the School Year

As you can see, there are many ways to incorporate choice into your classroom. Some are simple; others, such as learning centers, will require more planning and structure. Don't feel as if you have to reorganize your classroom into learning centers immediately; start with one idea and build on your success. One of my favorite ideas comes from Jill Yates, a first-grade teacher. She points out that behavior problems tend to occur during transition times in the classroom, either between activities or when some students have finished their work and others haven't. At the beginning of the year, she and her students "brainstorm appropriate and acceptable activities basically titled, 'What Do I Do When I Am Done?' Some choices are always available, such as reading a book or drawing in their journals, but other choices are also acceptable especially as all work is completed for the day. To help encourage and reestablish the wisest options, we are consistently highlighting those students who make those choices independently." What a terrific way to kick off the year with a focus on choice!

Summary

- By giving students a choice in your classroom, you increase engagement and productivity.
- It is important to balance choice with reliable structure. The happy medium will increase student success and motivation.
- When contemplating whether to allow certain choices, ask yourself whether the choice is connected to the current topic, on an appropriate level, understandable, original, and thought provoking.
- Through activities such as learning centers, alternative assessments, independent reading, and authentic projects, you can incorporate the choices your students need and want into your classroom.

If You Would Like More Information...

This site provides information about student success with choice in developing homework. http://www.education-world.com/a_curr/curr373.shtml

The Classroom of Choice: Giving Students What They Need and Getting What You Want by A. Erwin. & C. Jonathan, Association for Supervision and Curriculum.

Letting Children Take the Lead in Class, Education Journal by Ana Maria Andrade and Delia Hakim, Association for Supervision and Curriculum.

"What Choice Do I Have?" Reading, Writing, and Speaking Activities to Empower Students by Terry Bigelow and Michael J. Vokoun, Heinemann.

D

Data: More Than Numbers

If anything concerns me, it's the oversimplification of something as complex as assessment. My fear is that learning is becoming standardized. Learning is idiosyncratic. Learning and teaching is messy stuff. It doesn't fit into bubbles.

Michele Forman
2001 Teacher of the Year

When I talk with teachers about data, I hear a variety of comments. The most common is, "Yes, we have test scores. But shouldn't it be more than that?" Absolutely. As Michele Forman points out, we tend to oversimplify learning. Achievement is more than a test score, and data is more than a set of numbers. Data is any information that helps you understand your students and teach them more effectively. The purpose of data is to help you improve your teaching and your students' learning.

Formal Data

You probably have some formal data about each of your students. It might be from a standardized test or some other assessment that is collected in your school or district. The first step is to learn what information is available to you. Start by checking the cumulative folders of your students. Also, think of the people in your school who might know sources of data. For example, one of my graduate students was frustrated by the school's lack of information about one of his students. However, the second-language learning teacher was able to provide additional diagnostic data from an alternate assessment, once my graduate student asked for the information.

Think About It

What data is available to you?

Next, organize the information in a way that is helpful to you. When I was teaching, I used a simple chart so that I would know which skills each of my students had mastered. I coded the boxes with either a check plus (total mastery), a check (mastery but review is needed), a check minus (partial understanding), or a minus (minimal or no understanding). Then I could group my students accordingly for review or enrichment lessons. Now, there are computer programs that can help you organize this information. The key is to put the data in a format that helps you.

Data Chart

Student	Skill/Objective	Skill/Objective	Skill/Objective
Paul	✓	✓+	✓+
Marisa	—	✓	✓
Julian	—	✓	✓

Informal Data

Teachers gather informal data about their students all the time. When you ask your students to write an autobiography or complete exit slips at the end of a lesson, you are gathering data about who they are and what they are learning. However, the most effective teachers are intentional about the types of informal data they collect. Kendra Alston, for example, starts each year by asking her students to write about their favorite teachers. By analyzing the characteristics of those teachers, she is able to discover some of her students' trigger points for learning. Then she applies that knowledge in her own teaching to better connect with each student.

I was recently at Scott's Branch High School and observed a similar activity. John Hildebrand, a first-year teacher, assigned his ninth graders a simple homework activity: Write about what is working in our class and what isn't. As he explained to the students, "Transitioning to high school is important, and I don't think class is going as well as it could." As an example, he pointed out that many students were not completing their homework. He made the assignment and told them he would be using the information to improve his class.

I then visited a fifth-grade class in the same district. Beverly Simon had gathered very specific data at the start of the year in order to understand her students' math knowledge. Using a chart, she asked students to list what they knew about math and what they wanted to know about math. Then she asked them to work together to create a math alphabet of terms. Using the chart, she learned which broad concepts they knew, and then she gained a deeper understanding of their true knowledge based from their math vocabulary. The interactive lesson provided a collection of informal data.

Data About Your Lessons

Another type of data is self-reflection on the effectiveness of your own teaching. Sometimes we are so busy that we don't slow down to think about what is working in our instruction. At the end of a class or presentation, I jot down the answers to three simple questions.

Reflection Questions

What worked?
What didn't?
What do I want to change next time?

I always thought about the answers to those questions, but once I became intentional and started writing them down, I realized there were some patterns to what worked and what didn't in my teaching. I used the information more effectively, which leads us to the next point.

Using Data Effectively

Simply gathering data isn't enough. You can collect information, but if you don't use it to help you teach more effectively, you've wasted your time. The goal of data analysis is to make decisions that improve your teaching and your students' learning.

One of the major assignments in my graduate classes is a research synthesis paper. It's quite challenging, partly because it is unlike anything my students have ever written before. During my first semester, I offered to meet with any student for an individual writing conference. About a third of my students scheduled a meeting. When I graded the final projects, I noticed that all the students who met with me earned higher grades. The next semester, I made the conferences a requirement, and I found that my students were more successful. I continued to monitor my students' work, asked them regularly whether they thought the conferences had helped, and used their feedback to adjust the conferences to make them more effective. That's the purpose of data: use it to help you make the best possible decisions.

Multiple Sources of Data

If you organize your data collection to include both formal and informal assessments, you will have a great deal of information from multiple sources. This can be confusing, particularly if you have conflicting information, such as a standardized test score for writing and a student's writing in your class. Perhaps a student's class work is excellent, but his or her test score is low. What do you do? Think of data analysis like a triangle: Those two pieces of information should be evaluated together with a third data point, your teacher judgment.

Multiple Sources of Data

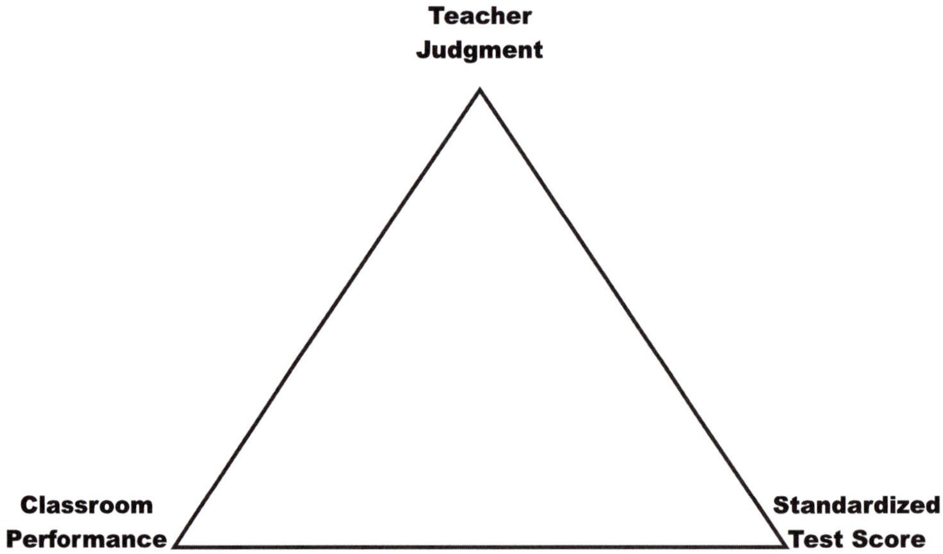

This is not a subjective judgment, such as "Oh, I like Shane, so I'll ignore the test score." Using your judgment means that you factor in your observations and knowledge of the student to determine the validity of the data. Perhaps you've noticed that Shane thrives in your class and particularly enjoys writing. He has told you that he enjoys your class because you allow him to choose his writing topics. During your first parent conference, Shane's father pointed out that his son worries about whether he is smart enough to go to college, so he stresses over standardized tests. Your own evaluation of this information tells you that Shane's score on the state writing test probably does not reflect his true ability. Again, data shouldn't replace your judgment; it should help you make decisions.

Making It Work

Using data effectively requires you to shift your thinking about its use. Data is more than a test score. Data is more than a number or a set of numbers. Data is any information that helps you learn about your students so that you can teach them more effectively. In short, when you focus on gathering and interpreting data,

DATA

D	Data helps you
A	Apply your expertise
T	To your students' individual needs to help
A	All students thrive

Summary

- Don't view data as judgmental. Instead, use it as a tool to improve your teaching and your students' learning.
- Gather information about your students early in the year from all potential sources.
- Put data in a format that works for you; you'll be more likely to refer to it if it is easy to understand and readily accessible.
- Use it! Avoid collecting data and then filing it away.

- Self-reflection is an extremely useful form of data. Continually stop to think about what works and what doesn't for each student.
- Multiple sources of data will give you a more rounded picture of each individual student.
- Data helps you apply your expertise to meet your students' individual needs. Then, all members of your class thrive.

If You Would Like More Information...

This site provides teachers with resources and research that supports the concept of looking at student work. http://www.lasw.org/

This site consists of an article on ways to use data in schools. http://www.educationworld.com/a_admin/admin/admin377.shtml

Using Data to Improve Student Learning in Middle Schools by Victoria L. Bernhardt, Eye On Education.

Data Analysis for Continuous School Improvement (2nd Edition) by Victoria L. Bernhardt, Eye On Education.

Using Data to Improve Student Achievement, Educational Leadership, February 2003

E

Expect the Best: High Expectations

Just when the caterpillar thought the world was over, it became a butterfly.

Anonymous

When I was in Columbus, Ohio, for a meeting, I had the opportunity to visit the Franklin Park Conservatory. While visiting the "Blooms and Butterflies" exhibit, I was reminded of the beauty of butterflies. I also remembered how much students are like butterflies. Just as butterflies are not in their final state when they are born or when they become caterpillars or even when they form a chrysalis, so our students are not in their final state when we are teaching them.

Think about that for a minute. Where are the students you teach? Are they newborn? Are they caterpillars? Or are they inside a chrysalis? What does that mean to you? If you think about your students as butterflies in the making, how does that change the way you view them? One of the most difficult things for teachers to do is to keep our expectations high, especially when our students' actions make us think less of them. There were days my students challenged me to come up with any positive thoughts about them, but those were the days they needed me most. I saw a comment one time on a bulletin board: Students need the most love when they least deserve it. I found that my students needed me to believe they were butterflies when they were most acting like worms!

> **Think About It**
>
> What does it mean to realize you are in the butterfly-growing business?

The benefit of high expectations is increased learning. There are three ways to incorporate high expectations in your classroom: through your words, through your actions, and through your expectations of one another.

Expect the Best Through Your Words

Have you ever thought about the difference that one word can make? Often, when I share ideas during a workshop at a school or in a school district, I'll hear this type of comment: "That's a great idea, *but* my students can't....*but* my students won't....*but* my principal wouldn't like that....*but* I don't think that would work in my class..." The word *but* can serve as a red light or a stop sign for progress. On the other hand, when I'm in a school that is making a difference with all of its students, regardless of age, gender, ethnicity, poverty level, or background, I hear this: "That's a great idea, *and* here's how I can make it work with my students." The word *and* is like a green light! As you work with your most challenging students, do you think in terms of *but* or *and*?

You might wonder why I'm focusing on teachers' language when we are talking about students. Your language reflects your beliefs, and your students follow your model. If they hear you using words as an excuse, so will they. And if your students are like mine, they have plenty of excuses; they don't need anyone to encourage them.

Another word to remove from your classroom is *can't*. Every time the word *can't* is said, it is like a weight that drags everyone down. I did not allow anyone in my room to say can't; it was one of our class rules. It was an important part of building a culture of high expectations. Anytime students began to say, "I can't do this," I would remind them of their strengths. This shifts the focus from the negative (what I cannot do) to the positive (what I can do).

Expect the Best Through Your Actions

Your actions reflect your expectations of your students. If you call on only the brightest students, you are telling your other students you don't believe they can respond. If you allow only certain students to participate in the science fair, the rest of your students learn that they aren't good enough to try. Therefore, it's critical to craft lessons and activities that require all students to demonstrate their understanding of the content. All of the chapters in this book provide examples of specific ways to involve every student in learning. I'd also suggest that you act on your higher expectations by giving students your BEST.

BEST

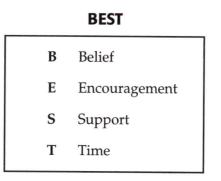

B	Belief
E	Encouragement
S	Support
T	Time

Belief

The most basic belief to convey to your students is a strong belief that they are important, valued, and capable. Diane Antolak, a high school principal in Fayetteville, North Carolina, explains that she personally reviews all student schedules. If she sees a student who has not registered for advanced classes, and she believes the student should be in a higher-level class, she will changes his or her schedule and then set up a meeting to discuss the change. As one student told me, "It makes me work harder because I know she believes I can do the work." Sharing your belief in a student is a powerful motivator.

Encouragement

Encouragement is the wrapping paper for your gift of belief. Students who do not have a lot of self-confidence need a steady stream of encouragement. Encouragement can be as simple as a smile or a few extra words written on a test, but it is always a signal to the student to keep trying. It's important to encourage students regularly, especially when they are not as successful as they could be. Focus on their strengths to give them the confidence to continue.

Support

Comments alone are not enough for your at-risk students. They also need you to take action to support their specific needs. This may be an action as basic as making sure they have the materials they need for class or a dictionary at home. We'll also explore more ways to provide extra help in Chapter H, "Help Me."

Time

Ultimately, inspiring students through your belief, encouragement, and support requires that you make a choice to invest your time in particular students. In fewer than five minutes per day, you can ask an extra question or make a positive comment several times during the day. The amount of time that you spend is not important, it your commitment to doing these things consistently with your students.

Expect the Best From One Another

Finally, it's important to provide opportunities for students to have high expectations for one another. Through your modeling, students can learn to reinforce positive actions for each other. Becky Serraglio, a kindergarten teacher in Charlotte, North Carolina, uses an interactive "Star Student of the Week" bulletin board. She explains, "Each week, a new student is named the 'Star,' and I decorate the bulletin board with anything that child wishes to display about himself or herself. Each day, we conduct a mini-interview of the child, during which he or she shares the items on the bulletin board. "The most valuable part of the Star Student activity is the writing exercise the students complete at the end of the week. I give each student a star-shaped piece of paper and allow them to write or draw one way the star student is special. I encourage the students to think of all the new things they learned about the student throughout the week. I use a shared writing prompt of '(Name) is special because...,' and the students complete the rest. Not only is this a meaningful writing activity for the students; but their creative responses are ones that are priceless in comparison with any word of effective praise an adult could use. For example, 'Raven is special because she helps me up when I fall' has so much meaning in an interaction between two children. I bind the writing samples together into a book for the student to keep at the end of the week."

Becky continues, "I was given confirmation that this activity was meaningful to the students when I observed a former male student, then a first grader, take out and open his homework binder to show me what was inside. Since the child had struggled with his behavior and often had a difficult time interacting with peers, I partially expected that he would show me a disciplinary note from his first grade teacher. Instead, I found his Star Student booklet, rumpled and worn from excessive use and reading, clipped to the back of his binder. He told me, over a year after the book had been made on his behalf, that he keeps it close to him as a reminder of 'how much other kids like him and think he is special.'" Becky creates an environment in which her students support each other and look for the positive. And because she rotates the recognition among the students, every child is affirmed.

Holding your students to high expectations is one of the most critical elements you can incorporate into your classroom. Many students do not have a vision of anything more than where they are right now. You can help them create a vision for themselves through your words, actions, and activities so that they support each other. Growing butterflies is hard work, but in the end, it is worth the time and effort.

Summary

- It is never too early to hold students to high expectations.
- Creating reasons why your students can't do something is a stop sign for their progress.
- Show students you believe in each of them by giving them your encouragement, support, and time.
- Build an atmosphere that supports high expectations by teaching your students to encourage one another and celebrate each other's successes.

If You Would Like More Information…

The 90/90/90 Schools: A Case Study by D.B. Reeves, Advanced Learning Press. Full text available online at: http://www.makingstandardswork.com/Downloads/AinA%20Ch19.pdf/.

Building Dreams: Helping Students Discover Their Potential by Mychal Wynn, Rising Sun Publishing.

Escalante: The Best Teacher in America by Jay Mathews, Henry Holt & Company.

Teaching What Matters Most: Standards and Strategies for Raising Student Achievement by R. W. Strong, H. F. Silver& M. J. Perini, Association for Supervision and Curriculum

Development.

Classroom Motivation from A to Z, by Barbara R. Blackburn, Eye On Education. (See chapter H).

F

Focus on Your Purpose

Alice is lost and asks the Cheshire Cat, "Which way should I go from here?" The Cat responds, "Where do you want to end up?" Alice says she doesn't care, then the Cat says, "Then it really doesn't matter which way you walk."

Lewis Carroll, *Alice in Wonderland*

Think About It

Reflect on a lesson that you taught today. Why did you teach it? What did your students learn?

How often do you feel you are focused on your priorities for instruction? In other words, how often do you feel as though you are pulled in a thousand directions instead of teaching what you have planned? That's a common sentiment. It's easy to become distracted by other important tasks, and then at the end of a week, semester, or year, we find ourselves saying, "What happened to the time? There were so many other things I wanted to do." In this chapter, we're going to look at two specific planning strategies: setting a vision and developing a blueprint for instruction.

Where Are You Going?

One of the strategies I recommend in *Classroom Motivation From A to Z* is to set your vision by writing a letter to a colleague. Fast-forward in your thoughts to the end of the year and describe what happened during the year. What did your students learn? What did they accomplish? How did they grow? By the end, you've described your vision, and in the process, you are reminded of your true purpose.

That is important because some of the critical things that you want to teach, such as independent learning, may not be on a skills checklist or a list of tested items. Therefore, it's easy to forget about them. We are so caught up in the urgency of busyness that important things don't happen. That's how I felt when I started teaching. I was so worried about covering the material for the test and making sure I finished the textbook that sometimes I didn't get to other important concepts. I quickly realized that many of the characteristics I wanted to develop in my students, such as working together, problem solving, and creativity, needed to be incorporated into my instruction. Otherwise, they would be leftovers—important lessons I would never have time for. That is the point: Unless you define and focus on your vision, you won't fulfill it.

Standards and accountability serve a purpose, but how you accomplish them is up to you. Anyone can meet the requirements, checking items off a list, but that won't promote higher levels of student understanding, nor will it encourage your students to be successful lifelong learners or problem solvers. But if you build your teaching around engaging instructional strategies, you will likely accomplish more—and your students will learn more, too.

Where Are You Now?

Once you have set your overall vision, how do you translate that into your everyday instruction? As you plan, you should ask yourself three simple questions.

Three Questions

Why am I teaching this?

What do I really want my students to understand or be able to do?

How can I get there?

Why?

Notice the order of the questions. First, start with your purpose for a particular lesson: Why are you teaching that specific content? Is it foundational knowledge that students need to understand in order to succeed in future lessons? Is the material something students will use in their own lives? A teacher recently told me that she was teaching the lesson because it was on the test. That is certainly important, but surely you can come up with at least one other purpose for your instruction.

During every lesson you teach, you should be able to answer the student who asks, "Why do I need to learn this?" And the answer should be relevant to the students, as opposed to "Because I said so." You can enhance your students' motivation by helping them understand the purpose of the lesson.

What?

Next, turn your attention to the content of the lesson. What do you want your students to know or do? This should be more than "pages 22–24." You have so much material to teach—what are the important parts? Some of the content in the textbook isn't necessary, and it's appropriate to skip those portions. But you need to think about what is important so that you can prioritize your teaching. Think about it this way: If I stood outside the door of your classroom and asked each of your students what they had learned in your class, what would you want them to say?

How?

Once you know why something is important and what your students actually need to know, then you can determine how to get there. A friend of mine says that you should always make sure you are using the right tool for the job. You shouldn't use a hammer when you need a screwdriver, or else the job won't be completed correctly. Textbooks, activities, and resources are all examples of your tools. You simply need to choose the one(s) that will help you accomplish your purpose. And you may need to be creative. The best tool for learning about the ocean might be an on-site field trip, but you may not be able to do that practically. In that case, you need to design ways to bring the ocean to your students, perhaps through a video or an online virtual tour.

Planning in Action: A Sample Map

When I was working on my PhD, I learned about a planning model from the Dupont Corporation.

The Task Cycle
Purpose (Why) → Product (What) → Process (How) → Resources

The Task Cycle focuses on the rationale (purpose) and desired result (product) before determining the process and resources that are needed. Think about how this would look in your classroom. Too often, we start with the process (how to get there) and resources (what we use). We plan to have students read about oil spills (process) in Chapter 5 of the textbook (resource). Then, we figure out what they should know at the end and how we'll assess their success. Let's take the same lesson, but this time, begin by recognizing that it's important for students to understand oil spills (purpose) and that they'll need to apply this knowledge in order to understand how clean-up costs and the environmental effects of oil spills (product) have an impact on their own lives. To do that, students need to read about oil spills (how), but the textbook (resource) includes only a short explanation. So, I also set up a lab activity that simulates an oil spill, and we read newspaper articles about actual oil spills that have occurred.

Try It!

Topic of Lesson/Standard:	
Purpose (Why do students need to learn this?)	
Product (What will successful learning look like?)	
Process (How will you teach this?)	
Resources (What resources do you need?)	

It takes time to plan using this process. However, if you want to influence your students' learning in ways that go beyond their preparation for the next test, it's imperative to think about your vision, the purposes of your lessons, and ways to help your students grow. Students who learn to work together are better employees; students who learn independently thrive long after they graduate. And if you want to ensure that your students learn what they need to know, then your lessons must support a clearly defined purpose. Be sure you know where you are going, and then design a clear map.

Summary

- Have a clear vision of what you want for your students, then build your teaching around engaging instructional activities that will accomplish your goal.
- Know why you are teaching a particular lesson, what you want your students to learn, and how you plan to get them to that point.
- Use the right tools to get the job done. Be creative in using all available resources to ensure that high-level learning is achieved.
- The primary focus in planning successful lessons is having a clear purpose and end product in mind. Only then can you determine what resources you'll need to use to get your students there.

If You Would Like More Information...

Understanding by Design, Expanded (2nd Edition) by Grant Wiggins and Jay McTighe, Association for Supervision and Curriculum Development.

Classroom Motivation from A to Z, by Barbara R. Blackburn, Eye On Education. (See chapter B).

G

Graphic Organizers

Students learn over half of what they know from visual images.

Mary Alice White
Teachers College at Columbia University

Think About It

How much information do your students comprehend when it is presented verbally? How much do they understand when they hear and see it?

We live in a visual society. And as Mary Alice White points out, our students learn visually. Graphic organizers help students visually organize information and encourage a deeper understanding of concepts. They can be used to teach almost any skill or concept, but we're going to look at several of the most common uses of visual organizers.

Weekly Vocabulary Study

Adam Myers uses a simple table in his vocabulary instruction. As he explains, "I want my students to feel comfortable learning new words on their own. My vocabulary chart has motivated my students to take an active role in learning new words. Before I designed this graphic organizer, I was that teacher who simply had his students copy a definition from the dictionary and memorize it for a quiz on Friday. Now, every week my students complete one of these charts while learning 15 new vocabulary words. If you consistently use the chart, students will know exactly what is expected of them throughout the week when studying vocabulary. Not only is it a consistent tool, but the best part of the chart is that it requires students to actively learn the words on variety of levels. While they are still asked to look up a dictionary definition, they have other ways of learning the word such as negating it, or drawing a picture in the clue box. Throughout the week, I help my students learn the words by practicing with fill in the blank sentences using the vocabulary words and offering them the chance to share their own sentences, clues, or definitions of what the word is and isn't. Since the vocabulary words that I choose come from the literature we read in my class, my students are not just excited to recognize a new word, but more importantly, they understand it as well."

Vocabulary Chart

Word	Dictionary Definition	My Definition or Clue	What the Word Isn't	Sentence

Graphic Organizers for Math Word Problems

Teachers at Chestnut Oaks Middle School in Sumter, South Carolina, faced a common problem. Some of their students were confident working with practice exercises in math, but they were unable to solve similar equations in the context of a word problem. Together, the teachers developed a graphic organizer to help their students break word problems into manageable chunks.

Organizing Word Problems

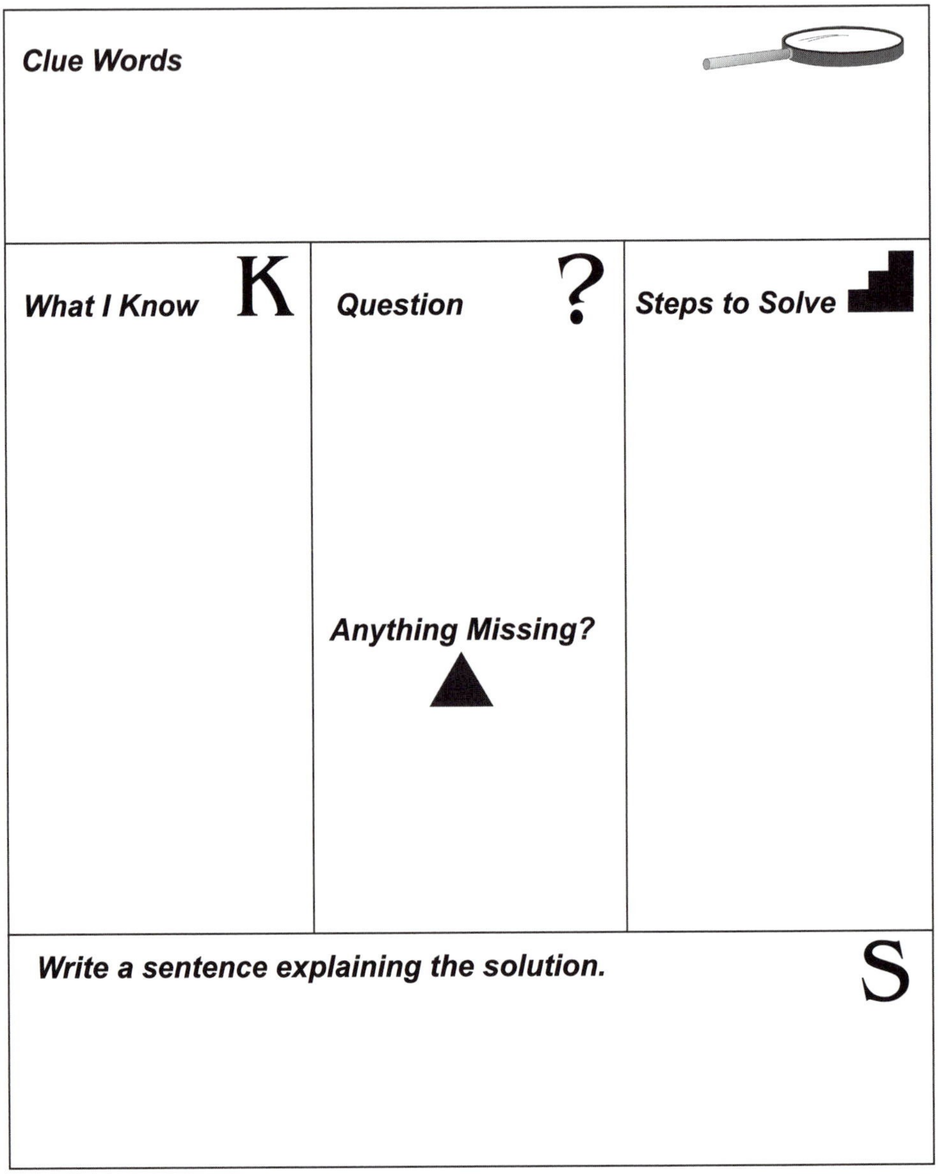

They systematically taught their students how to use the graphic organizer and provided multiple opportunities for practice. Picture codes were included to help students remember the steps easily.

Comparing and Contrasting

Graphic organizers are also helpful when you want students to compare or contrast information. The complexity of the organizer will depend on the nature of your lesson. For example, when I want students to see how two things are alike, I use a simple two column chart and list the characteristics of each. This works well for comparing basic knowledge about two habitats in a science class, two states or countries in a social studies class, two characters or two stories in a reading class, or two shapes in a math class. You can add columns to compare additional categories.

If I want to include similarities and differences, a Venn diagram allows me to visually see characteristics that are true for only one of the two categories, as well as those that apply to both.

Venn Diagram

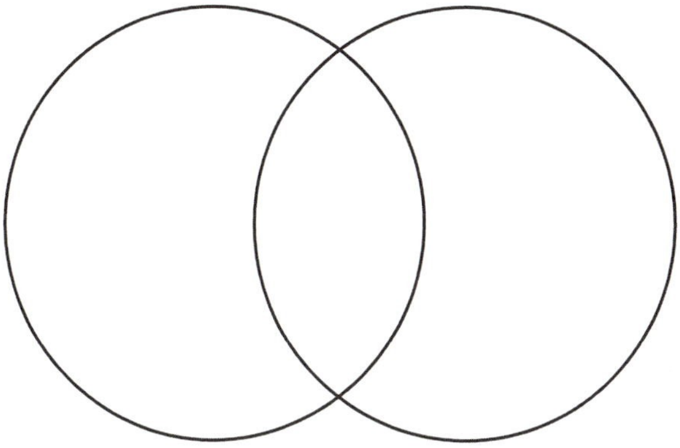

For more complex comparisons, you can use a table with structured headings. Once again, you can add rows or columns to correspond to the content of your lesson.

Basic Comparison of Shapes

	Number of Sides	Number of Angles
Square		
Triangle		
Circle		
Rectangle		

Character Analysis for a Play or Novel

	Personality Characteristics	How Character Connects to Main Character	Involvement in Plot	Comment, Action, or Dialogue That Best Reflects the Nature of this Character
Character				
Character				
Character				

As you can see, graphic organizers can be custom designed to match your content, regardless of what subject you teach or the age level of your students. You can also ask your students to create organizers for the information you are presenting. That process challenges them but also allows them to demonstrate that they understand the content.

Remember that the purpose of a graphic organizer is to help students understand the material; it is not to demonstrate that they can draw. Too often, we lose our focus when students spend too much time drawing organizers. Although you should have a variety of organizers, limit the number. The focus in your classroom is simple: Learn the material, not the organizers.

Summary

- In today's visual society, teachers must play to their students' natural strengths by allowing them to view information in a variety of ways.
- Graphic organizers put information in a visual format to help students deepen their comprehension.
- Use visual representations as a tool for learning, not as a method of memorization.

If You Would Like More Information…

This site provides templates of many different graphic organizers. http://www.eduplace.com/graphicorganizer/

Consistent, Coherent, Creative: The 3 c's of graphic organizers. By Baxendell, B, *Teaching exceptional children, 35*(3), 46–53.

Graphic Organizers for Writing, Incentive Publications.

Standards-Based Graphic Organizers Series from Incentive Publications (multiple subjects; sets for elementary and middle grades)

Content-Area Graphic Organizers Series from Walch Publishing (subject specific; designed for grades 7–12)

H

Help Me!

You must learn, you can learn, you will learn. The fact that you have not yet learned means that I have not yet found the way to explain the subject so simply, so clearly, and so exactly that it is impossible for you not to understand. But I will find the way. I will not quit on you.

Author unknown

Think About It

Do the students who need help ask for it?

In an ideal world, we would teach a lesson, and each of our students would understand the content and then use the information to achieve higher levels of learning. But that does not always happen. Some students immediately grasp the material and move forward, but others need additional assistance. That was true with my students. During my first teaching job, my students struggled with decimals. Math is not my strongest area, and as a first year teacher, I wasn't as effective as I could have been. My biggest mistake was teaching the same way over and over again. Somehow, I thought repetition would help. I knew it wasn't working, and they knew it wasn't working, but we kept working on decimal problems. Finally, in frustration, I went back to fractions, used examples from their lives (such as pizza slices) and related the fractions to the decimals. Then, my students and I saw success.

Providing appropriate extra help to students can be a challenge. First, there is pressure to make sure everyone moves through the curriculum in time for the test. Then, there are the times when you teach and teach and teach and just don't understand why your students don't understand. But that's the exact moment when they need you to keep going. If you are frustrated, imagine how they feel! There are seven key characteristics of effective support.

Effective SUPPORT

S	Structured
U	Understanding is the result
P	Personalized
P	Positive
O	Options within lesson and outside class
R	Repetitionless
T	Timeliness

Structured

First, effective support is structured. There is a plan to monitor student learning and provide extra help. Often, I'm in schools with extensive programs for tutoring, but all of the programs are optional. The students who need the most help don't always volunteer for assistance. Sometimes, they don't even realize that they need help.

If you build opportunities to assess student understanding at key points, you will be better able to provide immediate help to students. You can do this formally with a test, but that may be too late. Create ways to assess your students' understanding within each lesson or at the end of each class so that you can immediately address any concerns.

I used partner activities to do this in my lessons. After I taught a particular concept, I would ask students to turn to a partner and explain the concept. Then, the partners would share their understanding with another pair. Finally, I'd ask groups of four to write a short summary for the class, including any questions they might have. This made it safe for students to share information and ask questions.

Another easy way to assess is through the use of exit slips. As students are leaving your class, their ticket to get out of the door is a piece of paper with three sentences.

Exit Slip

What I learned today:
How this connects to something else I know:
A question I still have:

Exit slips allow you to quickly see what your students have learned and what they are confused about. And they are great tools to give you information to plan your next lesson. You can ask students to do this anonymously, or they can put their names on the slips so that you can work with individual students. Just be sure to have a plan. The structure will help you help them learn.

Understanding Is the Result

Effective support always results in a deeper understanding of the content rather than memorization of facts. As I learned, if a student does not understand decimals, more practice doesn't help. We need to find different ways to present the information so that students internalize what they are learning.

Christy Matkovich points out that teachers must find a way to deliver information to students "so their brains learn it. It might be drawing a picture or through movement. If your form of delivery isn't working, then find a different way to deliver it." Ideally, your lesson should include enough options for each student to learn in his or her own way. But if some students don't learn, then it's up to you to find a new way to help them understand.

Sometimes the best help comes from another student rather than the teacher. As science teacher Shannon Knowles explains, "I regularly have one student who understands explain the concepts to those who don't. Sometimes, they explain to everyone in class, sometimes to the one or two who need it. They just say it in a way that makes more sense to the students."

Personalized

Good support is also personalized to each student's needs. In order to customize your support, you'll need to learn as much as possible about every student. We'll talk more about this in Chapter U, "Understand Your Audience," but to connect with your students, it's important to learn about their interests, learning styles, strengths, and weaknesses.

Positive

It's also critical to provide support in a positive manner. Recently, one of my new graduate students was struggling with a research paper. She was returning to school after an extended break, and she found that doing research electronically was a new skill for her. After class, she made an appointment to meet with me individually for help. When she left my office, I thought everything was fine. One week later, she called me at home, quite upset. It seems that she did understand what to do, but when she tried to find research on her own, she struggled. She hesitated to call me because I'd already shown her how to use the online resources twice (once in class, once individually). We met the next day, and after we worked together, she immediately went to the computer lab to try it again on her own, this time with success. She was grateful and commented that I didn't seem to mind helping her again. Of course not. But if I had grumbled or said that she just wasn't paying attention, she would not have been as successful. Positive, ongoing encouragement of your students is a critical part of your role as a teacher.

Options Within Lessons and Outside Class Time

Effective support must be available during your lesson and outside class time. The most effective help comes during the lesson, when confusion is fresh in your students' minds. You don't want them to go home and practice something incorrectly. That is where sharing activities are helpful, they help assess and ensure understanding at multiple points during the lesson. But for those students who need extra one-on-one time, provide opportunities to meet with you after class. It is also common for a student to understand the material in class, but 24 hours later, he or she is confused. So it's important to be available to students at regular times. For example, the teachers at Willard

Middle School in Ohio post their office hours on their doors so that parents and students know when they can meet with teachers.

Repetitionless

In one of my workshops, a teacher said, "I know how to provide help for my students. Help means extra practice. The more help they need, the more homework I assign." That is not effective support. Repetition only works for memorizing isolated facts, and even that only provides short-term learning. Repetition rarely provides long-term learning. As Christy Matkovich says, "Practice needs to be quality. If the day didn't go well, if my students are lost or confused, then we'll just go home and start over the next day. If I send homework on a day like that, they'll create a way to do it, then we have to unlearn!" It's harder to "unteach" bad learning than it is to invest extra time in making sure that your students truly understand. If I don't understand something, practicing it over and over again isn't going to help. Hearing it again, told to me in the same words, only slower or louder, isn't going to help. Find ways to reteach information through learning centers or other hands-on activities.

Timeliness

Finally, effective support must be provided in a timely manner. If you wait two weeks after students ask for your help, you've lost your opportunity. Confusion is like a snowball rolling down a hill; it only gets larger. The longer you allow your students to be confused, the worse it gets. That's why you need to build effective structures to ensure that students who need help are able to obtain it immediately, thus preventing bigger problems later.

Create positive ways to support your students in your classroom to ensure their understanding at every step of the learning process. The time you invest will pay off as you see the light of understanding in your students' eyes.

Summary

- When you don't reach your students on the first attempt, try something new. If you continue to do the same things, you'll continue to get the same results.
- Structure your lessons so that immediate help can be given as students become confused.

- Students need positive, personalized help that results in true understanding of the content.
- Extra help should be offered at multiple times of day and presented in a different way than it was taught in class.
- Time is of the essence. Clarify misconceptions as quickly as possible.

If You Would Like More Information…

This site provides information about learning styles: http://www.ldpride.net/learningstyles.MI.htm

Scaffolding Language, Scaffolding Learning: Teaching Second Language Learners in the Mainstream Classroom, by Pauline Gibbon, Heinemann.

Scaffolding Learning by Jeffrey Wilhelm, Tanya Baker, Julia Dube, Heinemann.

Scaffolding Literacy Instruction: Strategies for the K-4 Classroom by Adrian Rodgers and Emily M. Rodgers, Heinemann.

I

I'm Listening...Or Am I?

I know that you believe you understand what you think I said, but I'm not sure you realize that what you heard is not what I meant.

Robert McCloskey

> **Think About It**
>
> How much of your instruction requires students to listen? Do you teach your students how to listen?

How important is listening in your classroom? The majority of our instruction requires students to listen, either to the teacher or to other students. But I've found that many students don't understand how to listen. We don't provide structured activities so that students learn how to listen. Simply lecturing and expecting students to absorb what we say isn't the best method of instruction.

Guidelines for Listening

First, we need to teach our students how to listen. I told my students there was a difference between hearing me and listening to me. If you don't pay attention to what I'm saying and process it, then you aren't listening to me. Our students today are so bombarded with sound from music videos and iPods that it's difficult for them to focus and truly listen to what you or their classmates are saying. As is true with any important information, you need to share some guidelines and then provide positive reinforcement when your students follow through.

Guidelines for Effective LISTENing

L	Look at the teacher or visuals
I	Intently focus rather than multitasking
S	Sit up and pay attention
T	Take notes or draw pictures to help you remember
E	Extend the information by making connections to what you know
N	Navigate your way to new learning

Active Listening

Next, we need to provide opportunities for our students to practice active listening. Barbara Liebhaber, a music educator at Moravian College, teaches her students how to listen. "The way to have students listen (active) rather than hear (passive) is to give them something very specific to listen *for* as they listen to a short example. [In my music courses,] I have found that students need to hear a listening example at least three times to really be able to pick out what they are listening for." The first time, she has them listen just to introduce themselves to the piece. The second time, she asks them to anticipate an element of the musical piece. Finally, the third time, she asks students to connect material "heard in the present to what was heard earlier in the piece as well as what will be heard later on. It is at this time that students actively listen and they are able to focus on what they were listening for." She provides a specific purpose for listening, as well as multiple opportunities to ensure success.

Fishbowl

We also need to create opportunities for our students to listen to each other. After students read a book or story, LaShana Burris at Cotton Belt Elementary School uses the "Fishbowl" activity to prompt discussion and encourage active listening. Three to five students are designated as fish, and they sit in a small circle. She gives them each a piece of food, which is an in-depth question. As fish, they need to discuss the answer to that question while another group of three to five students sit in a larger circle around them and listen to the discussion (thus the fishbowl). As she explains, "The people who are in the larger circle act as observers only. They use clipboards and paper to document a chosen fish's responses, behavior, and body language. After about five minutes of discussion, the observers share their notes with the fish they observed. After the last observer shares with his/her fish, fish and observers switch roles and the teacher throws in another question as a piece of fish food. It encourages all students to actively read for comprehension, it is a vehicle for shy students to begin to participate, and it builds community."

Morning Meetings That Spark Discussions

Jenny Johansson creates listening opportunities for her special education students through inquiry-based morning meetings. For the first 5–20 minutes of class, she focuses on independent inquiry. Students generate questions on a variety of subjects and read books and articles about their topics. "Then we get together in a circle on the floor for CPR [Circle of Power and Respect] for the actual meeting. During the independent inquiry time, they could sign up to actively participate in the meeting. The routine of the meeting includes a greeting, poetry, book recommendation, and inquiry sharing. During the greeting, they hear their name said in a positive light by their peers each day. During inquiry sharing students get to share with us what they are currently becoming an expert on. Student interests are really developed during this time." During the discussions, she enhances the student's listening through involvement and ownership. As she notes, "They are so motivated by their own voices being heard."

Paideia Seminars

Another type of discussion is a Paideia seminar, which shifts the role of the teacher to that of a facilitator and emphasizes each student's contribution to the discussion. As Marcia Alexander, a high school teacher explains, "Paideia seminar has been the most successful teaching tool that I have used because it gives students the opportunity to demonstrate their knowledge and concerns about an issue that they can relate to. For example, I may have students read an excerpt written by Sojourner Truth, an African American ex-female slave, abolitionist, and speaker of women rights. The discussion topic is discrimination and I create open-ended questions, such as 'Does being illiterate make a person less intelligent?'" In her role as a facilitator, Marcia ensures that every student speaks at least once before she poses another open-ended question. The nature of the discussion requires that students actively listen to each other in order to respond appropriately.

Listening as the Foundation

Whether you use lectures, discussions, small-group activities, or a blend of these activities, a basic element of success is that your students listen. I learned early in my teaching career that my students didn't always know how to listen, so I needed to teach them how to be good listeners. And then, I needed to provide multiple activities for them to practice the essential skill. Isn't that the key to any good instruction? Teach your students what to do and give them plenty of opportunities to apply the skill.

Summary

- Effective listening requires practice. Teach your students that hearing isn't the same as learning, a but concentrated effort to process what you are hearing enables learning.
- Listening isn't a passive activity. A student needs to be taught how to actively engage in verbal instruction.
- It is important to create opportunities for all students to become effective listeners.
- Allow students to talk about learning. It is beneficial and encouraging for students to hear one another speak.

If You Would Like More Information…

This site contains information about Paideia, the principles of instruction and results of Paideia education. http://www.cssd11.k12.co.us/springcreek/education_program/non_traditional_education/quintana's_classroom_philosophy/paideia_principles.htm

The Paideia Classroom: Teaching for Understanding by Terry Roberts and Laura Billings, Eye on Education.

Sing Along and Learn: Following Directions: Easy Learning Songs and Instant Activities That Teach Key Listening Skills, By Ken Sheldon, Scholastic.

Socratic Seminars and Literature Circles for Middle and High School English by Victor J. Moeller and Marc V. Moeller, Eye On Education.

Classroom Discussion: Strategies for Engaging All Students, Building Higher-Level Thinking Skills, and Strengthening Reading and Writing Across the Curriculum by Dixie Spiegel, Scholastic.

J

Just for Me

Winning on the scoreboard doesn't mean anything if all our players don't feel like they've had a fair chance to do their best on the court.

Bryan Gray
2005–06 recipient of the
Winnipeg Minor Basketball Association
Bruce Russell Coach of the Year Award

Differentiated instruction is a popular concept, and I have heard many interpretations of its meaning. For most teachers, it means creating lessons that include different elements to meet the needs of each individual student in a diverse classroom. According to the technical definition, in differentiated instruction, a teacher varies the content (what), process (how), or product (demonstration of learning) of instruction to enhance student understanding.

One concern I hear from teachers is that differentiation means some students will miss some aspects of learning. In sports, there are basic warm-up exercises and drills that every player does. But good coaches also work with each player during practice to increase strengths and bolster any weaknesses. During instruction, we need to do the same thing. We should teach the core information to everyone and adjust our lessons based on what we know about our students in order to help every individual reach his or her potential.

Basics of Differentiation

Two basic decisions need to be made in order to provide differentiated instruction. First, you need to decide what you are going to base the differentiation on. Do you want to differentiate based on learning styles, students' interests, or their skill development? That choice may change for different lessons. The second decision is how you plan to differentiate to match your students' needs. Let's look at several ways to differentiate your instruction.

Differentiating With Text Materials

When I taught at-risk students, I used a strategy called layering meaning to help them read and understand our social studies textbook. Because my students were reading below grade level, they struggled with our textbook. So I would find an article or section from another book on the same topic that was easier to read. My students would read that material first, which helped them build background knowledge and learn some of the specialized vocabulary. Then, when we read the textbook, they were more successful. As we progressed through the year, some of my students no longer needed the extra step. Others, however, needed the continued support. Therefore, I differentiated the reading assignments based on the skill level of my students.

Teachers in one elementary school that I observed had a different issue related to differentiation of content. About 75% of their students scored above grade level on state testing, and a large percentage of those students were in gifted classes. They were concerned that many of their students were not being challenged. The fifth-grade teachers typically chose one novel for all of the students to read each month. One teacher explained, "I'm not sure we're really meeting anyone's needs. The books are fun, but they are too hard for a few students, and I think they are probably too easy for a good portion of my students."

The teachers wanted to read a biography of Martin Luther King, Jr. Instead of choosing one book, we found four biographies at varying levels of readability. The students were then organized in groups based on their ability to read and discuss the novels. Each teacher met with one of the four groups to facilitate discussions and ensure understanding. Then, the students returned to their original classrooms and all of the teachers led whole-group discussions about Martin Luther King, Jr. A key element of this process was that each of the books contained some information that the other groups had not read. During the class discussion, the teachers asked questions to elicit specific information from each group.

One of the benefits was that even students in the lowest reading group had information to contribute to the discussion, reinforcing everyone's importance to the group. Students who could read at a higher level were challenged to do so. Finally, students were placed into new groups with others who had read different books so that they could create a final project about Martin Luther King, Jr.

Differentiating for Special Needs Students

Differentiation for special needs students should be based on their Individualized Education Plans (IEPs). As Susanne Okey, a former teacher explains, "Think of the IEP as a roadmap. It should be result of a huge diagnostic workout that shows holes and significant gaps in learning. Put [your IEPs] in your plan book so you see them every day with all your other goals, objectives, and standards. Cover them as you are teaching higher-level concepts with other students but don't eliminate higher-order thinking skills for this student."

For example, imagine that you are teaching your students how to write a three-paragraph essay. Sanchez's IEP goal is to write in complete sentences with appropriate capitalization and punctuation. How do you teach this while you are teaching others how to write an essay? Suzanne recommends, "You also want to start building the concept in him that writing is more than three short sentences. You might have him write a topic sentence for each paragraph. That might be bulk of his essay and he might work on that for period of weeks, but you don't want him to stay there. It's important to not stop and do a whole separate lesson for him. Don't exclude him from rich discussion; he may be able to take it in but not produce it."

Using Homework for Differentiation

Christy Matkovich differentiates homework in her math classroom. As you can see from the examples on the following pages, students receive the same type of homework and the same number of problems. However, students receive work that is customized to their understanding of the fraction concepts.

Why Did the Bee Become Frustrated While Calling His Mom?

Complete each word problem below. Locate your answer in the appropriate box. Place the letters located next to each word problem in the box that contains the correct answer. Put the letters together to form words that answer the riddle above.

GN 1. Max and his dad went to eat pizza after the high school football game on Friday. Max ate 1/4 of a pizza and his dad ate 2/3 of a pizza. How much pizza did they eat altogether?

AB 2. Sandy and her mother bought 1½ yards of fabric to make Sandy's Halloween costume. If they used ½ yard to make a collar for their new puppy, how much fabric was left for Sandy's costume?

AL 3. Patrick and Brandon are the best three-point shooters on their basketball team. In the last game, Patrick made ½ of the team points and Brandon made ¼ of the team points. What fraction of the team points did they make altogether?

ZY 4. Mr. Jones has two books about skateboards stacked on his desk. One book is 1/6 of an inch. The second book is 1/3 of an inch. How tall is the stack of books?

SI 5. The girls track team was practicing for the championship meet. Coach Barnes asked the team to run 1/4 of a mile as a warm-up. At the end of practice, they had to run 3/8 of a mile to cool down. What fraction of a mile did they have to run altogether?

UZ 6. In science class, students had to measure the length of two different lab tables. Both lab tables together were 2¾ meters long. If one lab table was 1½ meters, how long was the second table?

He kept getting:

1	1¼	½	5/8	11/12	¾
_____	_____	_____	_____	_____	_____

Why Did the Bee Become Frustrated While Calling His Mom?

Complete each word problem below. Locate your answer in the appropriate box. Place the letters located next to each word problem in the box that contains the correct answer. Put the letters together to form words that answer the riddle above.

GN 1. The football team went to eat pizza after the high school football game on Friday. One player ate 2/8 of pizza, another player ate 1/6 of pizza, and a third player ate ¾ of a pizza. If there were three pizzas, how much pizza was left for the rest of the team?

AB 2. Sandy and her mother bought 24/6 yards of fabric to make Sandy's Halloween costume. If they used 2/3 of a yard to make a collar for their new puppy, and 8/7 of a yard to make a baby costume, how much fabric was left for Sandy's costume?

AL 3. Patrick, Brandon, and Miguel are the best three-point shooters on their basketball team. In the last game, the team scored 108 points. If Patrick scored 2/9 of the points, Brandon scored 1/6 of the points, and Miguel scored 1/3 of the points, what fraction of the points did the boys score altogether?

ZY 4. Mr. Jones has four books about skateboards stacked on his desk. The length of the books are 10¼ inches, 113/16 inches, 9 3/8 inches, and 11¾ inches. How long would the books be if you laid them end to end?

SI 5. The girls track team was practicing for the championship meet. The girls team had to run a total of 9 miles during the whole practice. If they ran 13/8 miles for warm-up and 23/10 miles for their first drill, how many miles did they have left to run during practice?

UZ 6. Ms. Stevens placed all the science lab tables in a row. The row was 25½ meters long. Each table was 1 7/10 meters long. If Ms. Stevens removed three tables from the row of tables, how long would the new row be?

He kept getting:

11/42 ______	429/16 ______	513/40 ______	232/5 ______	15/6 ______	13/18 ______

Another way to differentiate homework is through the use of learning contracts. Christina Berry, a teacher at Andrews Elementary School, developed a reading homework contract for her students to complete. Over a six-week period, students must complete five items on the contract. In both cases, the teachers incorporate the essence of differentiated instruction, providing variety so that each student learns.

Third-Grade Reading Contract

I, ________________________, agree to read for 15 minutes every night and complete five of the following items by the end of six weeks. I will turn in this contract with the five items completed on ______________.

1. Write a summary of a book.
2. Read a newspaper article and write down the five W's of the article (who, what, when, where, and why).
3. Read a fairy tale and write a fractured version of the fairy tale. (Example: Cinderella's fractured fairy tale would be *Cinderella Skeleton.*)
4. Read a chapter book or picture book and change the ending of the story.
5. Draw a Venn diagram comparing one of the following:
   a. The main character with another character from the book
   b. The main character with a character from another book
   c. The main character with you
6. Illustrate four important events from a book.
7. Read a recipe or directions for how to make something and make it. You must bring the evidence to class (a picture of the item is OK), or you can write a summary of what you did.
8. Read a poem and make a list of adjectives that are used in the poem. Also list any similes and metaphors.
9. Complete a reading comprehension booklet.

I have chosen to complete ____.

I agree to complete the items I have listed above by the due date.

______________________________ (Student Signature) ______________ (Date)

I agree to remind students to work on their reading contract every day.

______________________________(Teacher Signature) ______________ (Date)

I will support and assist my student in meeting the terms of this contract.

______________________________ (Parent/Guardian Signature) ______ (Date)

As you try some of these ideas to enhance your instruction, don't forget the real purpose of differentiation. As Bryan Gray says in remark that opens this chapter, "Winning on the scoreboard doesn't mean anything if all our players don't feel like they've had a fair chance to do their best on the court." I would adapt that to say, school doesn't mean anything if all of our students don't feel as if they've had a fair chance to do their best in the classroom. Use differentiation to provide every student an opportunity to learn at his or her highest level.

Summary

- When differentiating instruction, you must make two important decisions: What purpose will the differentiation serve, and what methods will you use to accomplish it?
- Differentiation doesn't mean that all of your students are doing something different. By varying the complexity of the text, you can easily modify instruction while still teaching the same content.
- All students deserve the opportunity to participate in higher-level thinking activities. Differentiation simply means that some students may not answer certain aspects of the questions. But they are always given the opportunity to succeed.

If You Would Like More Information...

This site connects specific learning styles to teaching strategies: http://www.berghuis.co.nz/abiator/lsi/lsiframe.html/.

So Each May Learn: Integrating Learning Styles and Multiple Intelligences by Matthew J. Perini, Harvey F. Silver, and Richard W. Strong, Association for Supervision and Curriculum Development.

Fair Isn't Always Equal: Assessing & Grading In the Differentiated Classroom by Rick Wormeli, Stenhouse Publishers.

Handbook on Differentiated Instruction for Middle and High Schools by Sheryn Spencer Northey, Eye On Education.

Differentiated Instruction: A Guide for Middle and High School Teachers by Amy Benjamin, Eye On Education.

Differentiated Instruction Planner by Debbie Silver, Incentive Publications.

Classroom Motivation from A to Z, by Barbara R. Blackburn, Eye On Education. (See chapter V).

This site contains information on readability levels of books: http://www.lexile.com.

K

Kick It Up: Adding Rigor to Your Classroom

For people who don't understand as much...[they should] be in higher level classes to understand more [because] if they already don't know much, you don't want to teach them to not know much over and over.

Gabrielle, middle school student

Recently, I've read several news articles critical of schools and teachers. The authors usually comment on poor achievement linked to low expectations of students. In its 2006 report *Reading Between the Lines: What the ACT Reveals About College Readiness in Reading* (see http://www.act.org), the ACT reported that many students graduate from high school ill prepared for college-level reading or workplace literacy. And, as Gabrielle's quote reminds us, even some of our students view instruction as less than rigorous.

When I talk with teachers about increasing expectations, a common response is, "Our students are so far behind, we can't expect them to do even more." It is important to meet students where they are in order to help them move forward, but it is also critical that we expect students to learn at high levels. As I said in Chapter E, "Expect the Best," our first step is to increase our vision of our students' potential. Then, we need to raise our instruction and assessment to more rigorous levels.

In *Teaching What Matters Most,* Strong, Silver, and Perini define rigor as "the goal of helping students develop the capacity to understand content that is complex, ambiguous, provocative, and personally or emotionally challenging" (2001, p. 7). As you think about that definition, you realize that rigor is not just about difficulty. Rigor is also about helping our students learn to critically think about their learning.

Ways to Increase RIGOR in Your Classroom

R	Ratchet up the complexity of the task
I	Increase scaffolding
G	Guide your students
O	Offer questions and projects that stimulate open-ended thinking
R	Raise expectations for completion

Ratchet Up the Complexity of the Task

In order to increase the complexity of your assignments, shift your focus from isolated facts to the application of knowledge. Complexity isn't about doing more work, it's about doing less drill and practice and more higher-level thinking activities. Questions should be about how to do something or why something happened, not just what happened or when it happened.

A common activity in classrooms is to read a fictional story or novel. To increase the rigor of that activity, simply add a follow-up activity comparing the fictional text to nonfiction information. For example, if your students are reading the book *Who Really Killed Cock Robin* by Jean Craighead George, they can also research the environmental aspects of the story to determine whether the author was realistic in her use of detail in the story. Instead of simply reading and discussing the story, students are required to use research skills, cite sources, and compare and contrast information from a variety of sources. The new activity requires all students to think at a higher level.

Increase Scaffolding

When you raise the expectations in your classroom, you must also provide extra scaffolding for students. Simply expecting them to do more without additional support sets your students up for failure. I've included ways to scaffold instruction throughout this book, but let's talk about one specific strategy that is particularly effective when increasing the level of rigor in your classroom: multiple exposures to critical skills.

Some of your students will need several opportunities to learn higher levels of content. If the text material is more difficult, consider allowing students to listen to an audio recording of the material before reading it with the entire class. Or, some students might need to review the content in small groups using a Guide-o-Rama (page 113) while other students complete extension activities. You also might preteach content with students who need additional help, but it's important to find a nonthreatening way to do so.

One day, I tried an alternative method of preteaching with Roberto. He rarely volunteered to answer questions and generally was nonresponsive in class. Just before lunch, I asked him to stay and talk with me. I explained that on Wednesday, I would be teaching a new lesson, and I needed his help. We agreed to meet during study hall to go over the lesson together so I could make sure I was doing a good job. Then, I explained that I was particularly concerned about one of the questions I was planning to ask. I said that if no one answered it correctly, it would mess up the whole lesson. So we went over the answers, and he agreed to "help" me by raising his hand and responding correctly. Wednesday, Roberto was engaged throughout the lesson, offering answers and asking new questions. That one experience gave him the confidence to participate in later lessons. He also began to read ahead in our book to make sure he was ready for class.

Guide Your Students

As you scaffold instruction, remember that you are playing the role of a guide. You don't want to fall into the trap of doing the work for your students. As I teach my graduate students to research topics, one of our first activities is to discuss the characteristics of appropriate sources. Next, they find 15 research articles about a topic of their choice to bring to class. I take one student's set of articles and sort them into three stacks: appropriate sources, inappropriate sources, and sources that are acceptable with some limitations. Throughout the process, I talk through my thoughts (Are there references? Is there bias?) and ask students to help me decide how to categorize each article. Finally, the students pair up and sort one another's articles. Often, students will ask me to sort all of their articles. But I insist that they attempt the work first, and I look only at articles that are questionable. I've learned that if I sort all of the articles for them, they will never learn how to do it themselves. The same is true for your students. Model and provide guidance, but make sure they take ownership of their learning.

Offer Questions and Projects That Stimulate Open-Ended Thinking

Rigorous questions and tasks tend to be open ended rather than having one simple answer. Many students can complete numerical equations, until the equation is embedded in a paragraph that requires them to think about how to use mathematical knowledge to solve the problem. As you create lessons, craft activities that require students to apply what they are learning in a variety of ways. Don't ignore the instruction of basic facts, but effective instruction always focuses on the use of those facts, not the memorization of them.

Shannon Knowles holds an "Invention Convention" for her science students each year. Using material integrated from all subject areas, her students must create a new invention. In addition to sketching, designing, and building a model, each student researches patent information to determine whether his or her idea already exists. They also write a description of the invention. The finished products are creative, and students must complete extensive research in order to ensure that their invention actually works.

Sample Inventions

Jonathan—Handy bottle dispenser that allows young children to pour 2-liter bottles with a handle instead of using two hands.

Catherine—Disposable doggie slippers that fit on your dog's paws before they go outside. When they come in, take them off, throw them away. and your dog's paws are clean.

Martha—Baby bottle holder that includes a weighted ring and allows the child's cup to sit inside. If you try to knock the cup over, it will not fall because of the weight at the bottom.

Joseph—Leaf picker that picks up leaves but not pine straw in flower beds.

Raise Expectations for Completion (Not Yet)

Finally, you can increase the level of rigor in your classroom through your assessments. I regularly hear from teachers who tell me they have high standards, explaining that any student who doesn't turn in homework or a project receives a zero. Although that policy may send a strong message about meeting deadlines, I believe that allowing students to take a zero reflects lowered expectations. It permits a student to get by without actually doing the work and says to the student, "You don't have to learn this."

In my own classroom, I use a grading policy with a three-part scale: A, B, and Not Yet. If my graduate students are unable to complete a project at an acceptable level (B or above), then they receive a Not Yet and revise their work. Many teachers use similar scales, usually adding a column for a C. Grading rubrics can be used with any subject area, as you can see from the sample rubric for interpreting music data. When you require students to finish an assignment at an acceptable level, you show them that you believe they can complete the work.

Increasing the rigor of your instruction will challenge you and your students, but the results are worth it. Spend less time reviewing basic facts and more time teaching new concepts. Over time, your students will learn at a higher level and their problem-solving skills will increase.

Summary

- Meet students where they are, but expect them to grow to heights they've never imagined.
- Less is more. Give students small amounts of focused work that requires them to apply knowledge and evaluate information.
- You must support your students when asking them to complete rigorous tasks. This means giving them the tools they need to be successful but not holding their hands all the time.
- Don't set a ceiling on expectations. When you give students the freedom to explore and opportunities to be creative, they will often go above and beyond what you had planned.
- Expand your students' horizons by asking thought-provoking, open-ended questions.
- When you expect success at a high level, don't accept less from your students by giving them zeroes.

Unit VI Louisiana's Musical Landscape
Lesson 1 Music Around the State: Sound and Place

Louisiana Voices Folklife in Education Project
www.louisianavoices.org

Interpreting Music Data Rubric

Title/Topic **Louisiana's Musical Landscape** **Name** ________________ **Date** ________

Task: Complete the *Musical Elements Chart,* the *Music Genres and Venues Worksheet,* and the *Music Prove It,* and present information you learned in mural, poster, oral or written report, timeline, map, skit, or game.

Performance Element	Outstanding 20 pts.	15	Great 10 pts.	5	Not yet 0 pts	Possible	Actual
Discrimination	• Listened attentively; related musical excerpts to regions of the state.		• Listened to musical excerpts, but did not relate all of them to regions of the state.		• Not attentive during listening activity; relied on others to relate music to regions of the state.	20	
Identification	• Identified all musical elements present in excerpts, identified cultural practices that affect music.		• Identified some musical elements in excerpts; cultural practices that affect music not defined for all excerpts.		• Could not identify musical elements or cultural practices.	20	
Interpreting Information	• Categorized musical excerpts using all six musical elements; compared and contrasted recordings; recognized cultural characteristics that determine musical style.		• Categorized musical excerpts using most of the musical elements; most comparisons and contrasts were relevant; recognized some cultural characteristics that determine musical style.		• Information has not been interpreted; jumps to conclusions without carefully categorizing characteristics.	20	
Describing	• Used appropriate vocabulary to describe all genres and musical elements heard in musical excerpts.		• Described most genres and elements; some descriptions not appropriate.		• Used inappropriate descriptions for genres and elements.	20	
Disseminating Information	• Designed and created a mural, poster, oral or written report, timeline, map, skit, or game that effectively interprets the relationship of genres of music to Louisiana regions.		• Designed and created a mural, poster, oral or written report, timeline, map, skit, or game to interpret the relationship of genres of music to Louisiana regions, presentation lacking in clarity.		• Mural, poster, oral or written report, timeline, map, skit, or game not completed.	20	

Bowman, Paddy, Maida Owens, and Sylvia Bienvenu. "Interpreting Music Data." Louisiana Voices Educator's Guide, www.louisianavoices.org, Unit VI: Louisiana's Musical Landscape, Lesson 1 Music Around the State: Sound and Place. 2003.

If You Would Like More Information...

This site contains the report *Reading Between theLines: What the ACT Reveals About College Readiness in Reading.* http://www.act.org/path/policy/pdf/readingreport.pdf#search=%22reading%20between%20the%20lines %2C%20report%22

This site contains the report *The Silent Epidemic: Perspectives of High School Dropouts.* http://www.gatesfoundation.org/nr/downloads/ed/TheSilentEpidemic3-06FINAL.pdf#search=%22the%20silent%20epidemic%2C%20perspectives%22

This site includes rubrics that utilize Not Yet. It also describes many photos, essays, articles, virtual books, study guides, and other helpful resources relating to Folklife in Louisiana. The information can be adapted to many content areas. http://www.louisianafolklife.org/main_contact_link.html

Getting Students Ready for High School Series (set): http://www.sreb.org/main/publications/catalog/CatalogDisplaySub.asp?SubSectionID=42SREB/.

This site contains a rigor ad relevance framework for classroom teachers: http://www.leadered.com/rigor.html/.

Fair Isn't Always Equal: Assessing & Grading In the Differentiated Classroom by Rick Wormeli, Stenhouse Publishers.

Teaching What Matters Most by Richard Strong, Harvey Silver, and Matthew Perini, Association for Supervision and Curriculum Development.

Classroom Motivation from A to Z, by Barbara R. Blackburn, Eye On Education. (See chapters R and S).

4

Literacy for Everyone

Reading and writing are the wings that lift students to new levels of understanding.

Barbara R. Blackburn

Think About It

Are you a literacy teacher?

How did you answer that question? Here is my answer: Everyone is a literacy teacher. If you teach math or another subject rather than language arts, you might think, "I need to skip this chapter. Teaching reading and writing is not my job." Let me explain. I'm not saying that you need to stop and teach a mini-lesson on how to read or write. However, if you want your students to understand your content, and if you want them to demonstrate an understanding of your lesson, they will need to read and write. Our focus in this chapter is literacy as a tool for understanding—using reading and writing to support learning.

Modeling

The first action you can take as a teacher is to model literacy for your students. Simple actions can make a difference. For example, I brought a newspaper to school with me everyday. I scanned the headlines, and if anything related to what we were learning, I would use the newspaper article in the lesson. One day, I overslept and didn't stop to buy a paper. All day, my students asked me what was wrong because they noticed I didn't have a paper on my desk. That's when I realized that, for many of them, I was the only person they knew who read a newspaper.

You can also talk about the books and magazines you read or how you use writing in your life. Make sure your students see you using a dictionary or researching information on the Internet. Every semester, my graduate students share stories about their students' reactions to the realization that their teacher has homework, too. It's certainly an eye-opener for the students and sends a message about the importance of lifelong learning. If you have a guest come to your class, always ask the speaker to explain how reading and writing is a part of his or her job.

A Literate Environment

It's important to have a physical environment that supports literacy. Ideally, every classroom should have age- and content-appropriate reference materials (dictionaries, thesauri, etc.) and a classroom library of reading materials for student use. This can include magazines and other real-life reading material tied to the subjects you teach. If possible, have a designated "writer's corner" or reading area where students can curl up with a good book.

In Erin Owens's first-grade class, her students have multiple opportunities and supports for writing. "They have science and social studies journals separated by themes, mental math notebooks, pen-pal journals, a creative writing center, and writing portfolios. Students are always discussing and writing about our learning."

Comprehension Strategies

We often ask students to show their understanding of material they have read or heard. This can happen in a way that is boring, or you can be creative and add spice to your classroom.

Katrina J. Smith, a third-grade teacher at St. James Elementary School, uses her school's READSUP strategy to help students understand a selection of text.

READSUP

R	Read the title and questions.
E	Encircle key words in the questions.
A	Always read the selection carefully.
D	Did you write the main idea?
S	Select the best answer.
U	Underline to verify your answer.
P	Put the number of the question when you verify.

Mary Sanford, a teacher of students with special needs, adds flavor to her lessons with M&Ms, which typically have six colors of candy. She puts some of the candy in a small cup, and students choose a piece of candy and do the corresponding activity. This allows student to "practice up to six strategies, review six terms, or share information in an ice breaker activity. The whole activity can be used as a warm up or review, and it takes as little as 5 minutes or you can stretch it to 15 minutes." This activity can be done individually, in pairs, or in small groups and can be adapted to almost any subject area.

M&Ms Activity

BLUE—Tell the word or words that are important or unusual.

GREEN—Ask a question of the author or the text.

ORANGE—Clarify: Put ideas in your own words.

BROWN—Visualize: See in your mind what the writer is describing.

YELLOW—Predict: Think about what will come next.

RED—Relate to what you have read: Give an opinion, reaction, or connection.

Kendra Alston, an academic facilitator, uses a countdown activity at the end of the day. Using posters or overhead transparencies, she asks students to complete the prompt, starting at five and counting down to one. It's a quick way to review material and gauge the level of your students' understanding.

Five Golden Lines

5	Interesting phrases from the text
4	New vocabulary terms and your personal definitions
3	Key points
2	Your own ideas about the subject
1	Question you still have

Writing to Demonstrate Understanding

Writing is an excellent way to determine whether students understand content. I regularly use exit slips in my classroom (see Chapter H). At the end of class, I ask students to write down something they have learned and a question they have. I can scan these quickly to see whether I need to review material during the next class. It also allows students to ask me questions privately.

I also like to use a "pizza wheel" to review material that students are assigned to read before class. Each student writes a fact that he or she learned on one of the pizza slices. Then, working in small groups, students pass their papers to the next group member, who also writes a fact. This continues around the circle until each pizza is full. Students can discuss the material, using the pizza wheels as a prompt.

Pizza Wheel

Student: ______________________

Topic: Volcanos

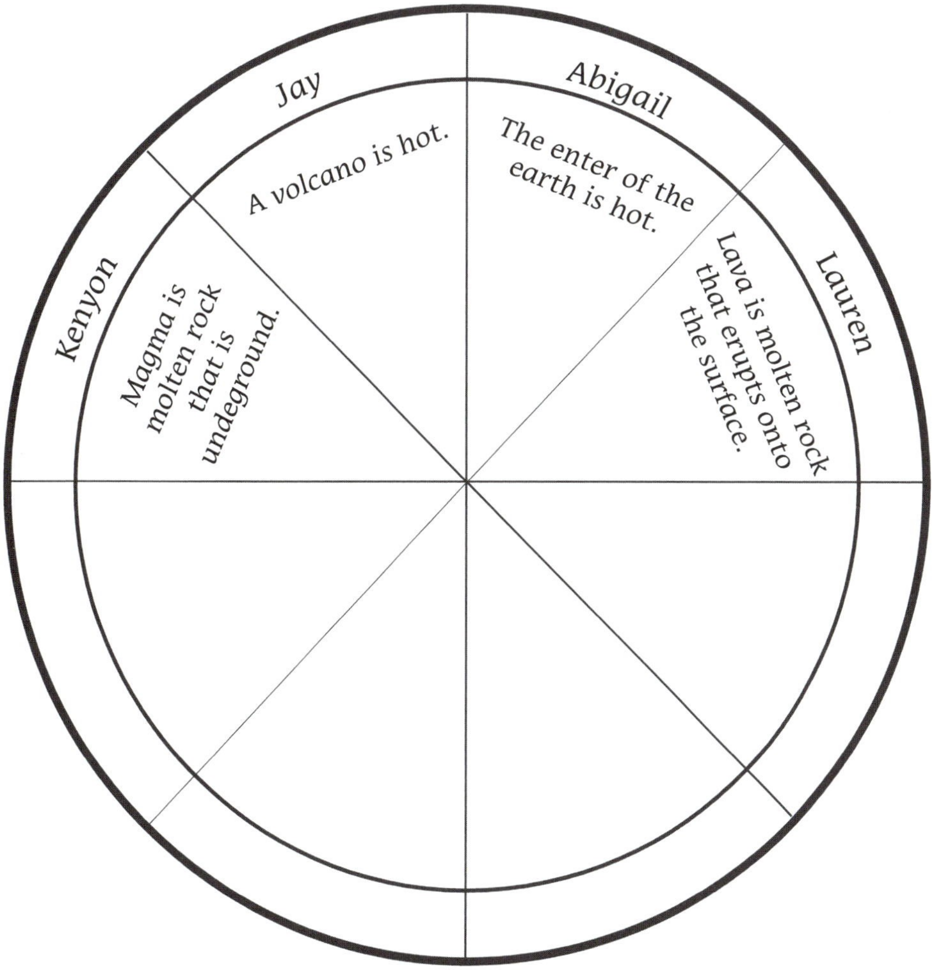

Although you can measure your students' understanding in an oral discussion, asking each student to write his or her response ensures that all students are involved in the lesson and provides an opportunity for every student to respond. Integrating literacy into your classroom facilitates understanding. Use reading and writing to help your students learn, and watch them soar!

Summary

- If you educate students of any age, you are a reading and writing teacher.
- Model the practice of reading for your students; it sends a powerful message about the importance of literacy.
- Make your classroom a literate environment. Include of variety of text materials for reading and tools for writing.
- Comprehension strategies help students monitor their reading and check for understanding. Spice up reading assignments in your classroom by trying out creative, engaging reading strategies.
- A student's written response to a text or a class discussion can be an accurate indicator of understanding. Use writing to check for clear comprehension.

If You Would Like More Information...

These sites contain information on teaching literacy skills: http://www.infolit.org/and http://www.reading.org/.

Nonfiction in Focus: A Comprehensive Framework for Helping Students Become Independent Readers and Writers of Nonfiction, K – 6 by Janice Kristo and Rosemary Bamford, Scholastic.

Active Literacy Across the Curriculum by Heidi Hayes Jacobs, Eye On Education.

Strategies That Work: Teaching Comprehension to Enhance Understanding by Stephanie Harvey and Ann Goudvis, Stenhouse Publishers.

Read & Write it Out Loud! By K. Pollette, Pearson Education, Inc.

How to Write a Great Research Paper by Leland Graham and Darriel Ledbetter, Incentive Publications.

How to Teach Reading if You are Not a Reading Teacher by Sharon Faber, Incentive Publications.

Classroom Motivation from A to Z, by Barbara R. Blackburn, Eye On Education. (See chapter L).

M

Making It Real

Make It Real

I just don't see the point in why I need to know this junk
You say if I don't learn it, then surely I will flunk
But I need a better reason for learning all this stuff
It's boring and it's pointless, so learning it is rough...

Annette Breaux

> **Think About It**
>
> From your students' perspective, how relevant is your instruction?

Have you ever heard a student ask, "Why do we need to learn this?" I've been asked that question more times than I can count. And too often, I hear teachers answer, "Because it's on the test" or "Because I said so." Those simply aren't the best answers to the question. I've found that we all have a radio station playing in our heads: WII-FM, What's In It For Me? Just as you ask that question when you attend a meeting or a workshop, your students ask it every day in your class. What is in this lesson for me? Why should I pay attention? Making learning relevant for your students means making it *real* for them.

REAL Learning

R	Relevant
E	Engaging
A	Application to
L	Life

Relevant

In most lessons, simply giving students an example that they can relate to their own experience will enhance the lesson. If you are teaching about map skills, you can have students draw maps of their classroom, their school, or their neighborhood. One of my favorite picture books is *Measuring Penny.* The main character is assigned a project by her teacher to measure something at home. She chooses to measure Penny, her dog. The book is a excellent example of a real-life project that inspires a student.

Donna Gillespie teaches spreadsheets to her high school students. To make the lesson relevant, she asks them to create a simple budget. In a follow-up, they are required to calculate grades. Donna explains, "Some of them liked giving grades so much they said they wanted to become a teacher. Others said, 'Do you have to do this all the time with our grades?'" As the students created a grading system, they understood how their own grades were calculated in their classes. They were immediately able to make a connection to their own experiences.

Grading Project

You are a high school computer applications teacher. The compiled grade for your students is made up of 30% unit test grade, 30% major project grades, and 40% class work.

During the course of nine weeks, you give three unit tests, assign two major projects, and grade 12 class work assignments. In this class, you have 20 students. You are to create a spreadsheet and calculate grades for each of the students in your class. Use function formulas to calculate the average in each column by including the grade column, the lowest grade in each column, and the highest grade in each column.

Jill Mailler uses popular music to teach her sixth graders difficult concepts. As she explains, "To teach irony, I use Alanis Morissette's song 'Ironic.' Music is a great way to relate concepts to students in a way that is meaningful to them. It works!" Her students respond to her use of "their" music in her class.

Engaging

To engage his students more actively in learning, Scott Bauserman, a social studies teacher in Indiana, uses mock courts. The intent is to "help students understand the American judicial system, justice, fairness, looking at evidence and circumstances from multiple perspectives, and plain old logical thinking." As he explains, "I built a case around the story of the three pigs. I had the students construct the story of the three pigs as they knew it. I had them read the 'politically correct' version of the three pigs, then we read the wolf's perspective from *The True Story of the Three Pigs* by A. Wolf. Students were prosecution attorneys, defense attorneys, the defendant, the judge, a bailiff, a court reporter, or a witness. No student could be a juror. All students had to participate in the trial, which was videotaped for other classes to view and decide on the guilt of the wolf."

Similarly, Eileen Ball uses active involvement to help her elementary students better understand history. "As my class studied the time leading to the American Revolution, we discussed the taxes imposed upon the American colonists by the British. We discussed how unfair the colonists thought the taxes were, and how the British felt it was unfair to be taxed for the French and Indian War which did not help British citizens. To make this real to my students, half of them were labeled British citizens, and half American colonists. Each was given paper money (pence or cents) which were spent on 'taxes.' The British were able to vote on their taxes and the American colonists were able to boycott their taxes." As students become a part of such lessons, they are more apt to remember and apply the learning.

Application to Life

To help his math students apply learning to their lives, Chad Maguire challenges his students to complete a numeration scavenger hunt each year. In the introduction to the assignment, he tells students, "When you buy a car, follow a recipe, or decorate your home, you're using math principles. People have been using these same principles for thousands—even millions—of years, across countries and continents. Whether you're sailing a boat off the coast of Japan or building a house in Peru, you're using math to get things done."

"Very few people, if any, are literate in all the world's tongues—English, Chinese, Arabic, Bengali, and so on. But virtually all of us possess that ability to be literate in the shared language of mathematics. This shared language connects ancient scholars to medieval merchants, astronauts to artists, peasants to presidents, and ancient Greece scholars to you. In this project we will explore how math concepts and numeration are used in everyday life. You may put the items together in a scrap book, notebook, on a poster, or any other format you may think of."

Sample Scavenger Hunt Items

- Dimensions in inches (length and width) of the newspaper
- An advertisement for 20% off
- An article from the sports page with some kind of statistic
- A fraction printed in a newspaper or magazine
- A food nutrition label that shows 2 grams of protein
- Picture of a dozen of something
- Title of a song with a number in it (and artist)
- Book with a number in the title (and author)
- Number of points a football team has if they score a touchdown, an extra point, a safety, and a field goal
- Sum of all the ages of the members of your immediate family
- The Roman numeral for 5,000
- Three nursery rhymes with the number 3 in the title
- The three-digit number in the Dewey decimal system for individual biographies
- Number of squares on a standard checkerboard
- Number of fluid ounces in a gallon of milk
- Picture of a person wearing a shirt with a number on it
- Number of miles from your house to the school
- A coupon for 25% off
- A picture of an automobile license plate with the number 5 on it
- A picture of a clock showing half-past the hour
- Picture of a speed limit sign with the number 5 on it.
- The number of pages in your math textbook. Count all pages!

One year, I taught reading using the state driver's manual. Several of my students who were reluctant readers needed to understand the manual in order to pass a test to receive a driver's permit. It was interesting to see their high level of engagement because of the immediate application to their lives.

Jason Womack points out that connecting with real life is also about using students' current experiences to facilitate new learning. "When I was working with a student group on World War II and postwar testing of nuclear and atomic devices, I had a group of students [in Southern California] who were surfers. One of the assignments that I gave for this group of students was to go and find out what the surfing was like through the 1950s and 1960s, which was when it was just starting in that community. A lot of students came back and said they did not realize how much damage was done in the Pacific Ocean around nuclear testing and atomic testing." His purpose wasn't to make a judgment on whether the decisions about testing had been good or bad; he wanted his students to connect his instruction to their daily life. And that's what making it real is!

Summary

- Real-life instruction means real life to your students.
- Make your activities relevant to students' lives.
- Create engaging lessons that involve your students.
- Real-life lessons also apply to your students' experiences, both current and in the future. Get to know them and link your activities to their interests and goals.

If You Would Like More Information...

This site provides strategies for teachers to authentically engage students in a mathematics classroom. http://www.ncrel.org/sdrs/areas/issues/content/cntareas/math/ma300.htm

Increasing Student Learning Through Multimedia Projects, by M. Stimkins, K. Cole, F. Tavalin, & B. Means, Association for Supervision and Curriculum Development.

Motivating Students Through Project-Based Service Learning by Melanie Bradford, T.H.E. Journal, 32(6).

N

Next Steps (Helping Students Break Down a Task)

How do you eat an elephant? One bite at a time.

African Proverb

> **Think About It**
>
> Do you have students who are overwhelmed during class? How do they respond when that happens?

There were times when my students were so overwhelmed with a task or lesson that they shut down. They saw no possibility of success because they didn't even know where to start. I was reminded of this feeling when I was in a store looking at puzzles. One of the boxes had a large heading that read, "Extra-Challenging!" This particular puzzle was unique. You were not given a picture of what the finished picture would be; therefore, you would have to guess as you tried to put together 1,000 pieces. I don't know about you, but attempting to match pieces without having any idea as to the design is not my idea of fun. Yet that's exactly what we ask students to do with new learning. Our mode of instruction says, "Trust me. I know where we are going, so you don't need to." But students don't always respond positively to that approach.

Start With the End

This is true when students do not know what good looks like. We ask students to complete an assignment, and we are frustrated when the quality of work does not match our expectations. This leads us to question whether the student cares about doing the work or whether he or she even tried at all. But many of our most frustrated and frustrating students simply don't know what to do or how to do it, or they may think that what they are doing is right. The solution to this issue is simple. Show them samples of final products, explain what you are looking for, and give them opportunity to self-assess.

John Hildebrand, a social studies teacher at Scott's Branch High School, follows this process with his ninth graders. He requires his students to write a proposal for a book report. As I visited his classroom, he explained to his students, "I won't ask you to do something I won't do. So, I'll be doing each step with you." He reminded them that the proposal should include the title and author of the book and a link to a specific social studies theme from the state curriculum. Then, he read them his own sample proposal. His students had a clearer picture of the assignment when he finished.

Chunking Content

For most of my students, note taking was a chore. They either wrote down everything I said or nothing at all, and I did not understand the problem. I thought they were either perfectionists who wanted to write down everything, or they were simply disengaged and did not want to take notes. For most of my students, neither was true. They simply were overwhelmed with the process of taking notes, whether from my instruction or a book.

I began to teach them to use a basic note-taking format with two columns. On one side, I provided an outline of the main topics I would teach, and students took notes about each point on the right. For more structure, I sometimes put the number of points they should have on the right side. For example, when I taught the symbols of North Carolina, the right side had 12 bullets, so they knew to listen for 12 symbols.

It's also important to chunk material when asking students to complete bigger projects. When Kendra Alston wants her middle school students to write a paper about media piracy, she starts with a one-minute essay. Students are given an index card and one minute to write an essay about problems. Over a period of several weeks, she continues to do short writing assignments with her students that link together to form a larger essay. Her students don't see the big assignment as hard because they've done so much of the work one step at a time.

Using Visuals

Many teachers use visuals to help their students remember steps in an activity. Desirae Remensnyder provides key information for her science students. "I have a reminder board in the back of my room that highlights the important items for each lab. I list the safety equipment needed, proper disposal methods, etc. We review the highlights before the lab, and the reminder board is right in front of them when they perform the lab."

Another way to use visual reinforcement is through the use of a color-coded timeline. This is particularly helpful when you are asking students to do a longer-term activity. My students struggled with activities that took longer than a day or two. They didn't seem to remember what we had done or how it fit into a bigger picture. One day, I put up a chart with color-coded steps and used a large arrow to pinpoint where we were in the process. It made a difference immediately, and they were more successful.

Skills Versus Processes

Missy Miles builds on that strategy but adds several specific elements to ensure her students' successful completion of a challenging activity. "To remain focused on my purpose, I put a sheet of chart paper on the bulletin board at the beginning of a new unit. I tell the students what they are going to be expected to be able to do by the end of the unit, and they tell me the skills they are going to need to master and the knowledge they are going to need to possess in order to be successful on the final assessment. This poster remains at the front of the room for all of us to see throughout the unit. At the end of each day or series of days, I revisit the chart paper and ask the students what skills we have covered that will help them on their culminating assignment. We check these off together if the class decides they feel comfortable independently using the skill. Or, we put a question mark if half of the students would like more modeling or practice with the skill. This system keeps us focused on why we are doing the things we are doing in class and where we are headed in the near future. It also helps them evaluate where they stand individually as far as being prepared for the project/test/written assignment at the end of a unit."

Her design not only helps students see the next step but also involves each student in creating the list of skills they need to use. She makes sure students understand that creating something—in this case, a project—requires both skills and knowledge. And she helps them see progress every day by checking off each item.

dents understand that creating something—in this case, a project—requires both skills and knowledge. And she helps them see progress every day by checking off each item.

Culminating Assignment

Research a controversial topic and present a persuasive speech that takes a stand on one side of the issue.

Skills Needed	Knowledge Needed
▪ How to narrow down a topic ▪ How to write a persuasive speech ▪ How to research a topic ▪ How to structure a persuasive piece ▪ How to deliver an effective speech ▪ How to include facts and statistics in my writing ▪ How to cite my sources	▪ Knowledge of the research of both sides of topic ▪ Elements of persuasion ▪ Elements of an effective presentation

Support Without Creating Dependence

It is important to help students understand the different steps that are necessary to accomplish a task and to be successful at learning. For many of our students, learning is like eating an elephant. What they see is too overwhelming for them, and they don't know where to begin. That's why it is important to help your students eat the elephant one chunk at a time. However, in the process, remember that the ultimate goal is student independence. So use these strategies to support your students, but help them learn the process. Then, on a future project, they will be able to break down the steps on their own.

Summary

- Students, like adults, need to know where they are headed. Clue them in on the final outcome of their learning.

- A student's productivity will be maximized if you show them what you expect.
- Break down a seemingly overwhelming assignment into small, manageable pieces.
- Acknowledge skills acquired throughout the learning process. Students should be constantly reminded that they are mastering skills needed for a culminating activity.
- The ultimate goal in teaching is to promote eventual independence. Begin to show students how to break down large tasks on their own.

If You Would Like More Information...

This site contains information on looking at student work: http://www.lasw.org

This site contains information on how to show students what good study skills look like: http://www.resourceroom.net/older/ida_studyskills.asp

A Facilitator's Book of Questions: Resources for Looking Together at Student and Teacher Work by David Allen and Tina Blythe, Teachers College Press.

O

Options for Successful Homework

I like a teacher who gives you something to take home to think about besides homework.

Lily Tomlin

Think About It

How do your students respond to homework assignments?

Homework is an issue for many students and teachers. In almost every workshop that I do on classroom motivation, a teacher will ask, "How do you motivate students to do homework?" Of course, the answer is complicated. You can make students do homework by increasing rewards or punishment, but that rarely works in the long term. The real solution is to create homework assignments that students are most likely to complete and then provide the support necessary to help them be successful. Effective homework is based on several key principles.

Effective HOMEWORK

H	Has a clear purpose
O	Opportunity for success
M	Makes quality the focus
E	Extends, reinforces, or previews content
W	Work is done independently or with appropriate support
O	Ownership felt by students
R	Receives feedback of some type
K	Kid friendly

Clear Purpose

Homework should have a clear purpose, and students should understand the purpose of the assignment or activity. During my first year of teaching, another teacher told me to assign homework every night. I didn't realize that by following her advice, I was teaching my students that homework is an item to check off a list, not something of authentic value. Homework is an extension of your instruction, so it should always have a specific purpose, just like your lessons (see Chapter F). As Shannon Knowles, a sixth-grade teacher says, "Explaining why I'm assigning the homework helps to get it done; I don't give homework just to give homework."

Opportunity for Success

Homework should provide students an opportunity to be successful. On one occasion, I was in an elementary school classroom watching a lesson on fractions. I'm not sure who was more frustrated—the teacher or the students. As the students became more confused, the teacher finally stopped and said, "This isn't working. Do the rest for homework." The students had absolutely no idea how to proceed, and their likelihood of success was minimal. As Christy Matkovich, a math teacher, points out, "If the day doesn't go well, if students are lost and confused, I just scratch through the lesson and we start over the next day. If I send home practice after a day like that, they'll create a way to do it, then have to unlearn what they did wrong." Don't waste your time or your students' efforts on work that offers no opportunity for success.

Focus on Quality

Homework is more effective when the focus is on quality as opposed to quantity. More is not necessarily better, particularly when students are just beginning to understand a concept. I once heard a speaker say, "Practice doesn't make perfect. Perfect practice makes perfect." That made me think about homework. If students don't understand how to do something but practice it 50 times, they will learn the wrong thing. I would prefer to give my students small opportunities to show me they understand so that I can build on that foundation in the future.

Extend, Reinforce, or Preview Content

Effective homework assignments extend, reinforce, or preview content. If students have mastered the material, you may choose to assign an independent project to enhance their understanding or allow them to apply their knowledge. After a unit on creating spreadsheets, you might ask students to build a budget using a spreadsheet. However, if students are just beginning to understand a skill, you may want them to complete additional practice to reinforce the knowledge. When I taught parts of speech, for example, I would ask students to find examples in newspapers or magazines and bring them to class. At times, my homework previewed upcoming content. For example, one day, I asked my students to make a list of places that they or their family had visited. The next day, when we discussed the regions of the state, we plotted their vacation sites on the map and categorized them by region.

Independent Work

Effective homework can be completed independently with minimal and appropriate support. If the assignment is too difficult, students are more likely to ask someone else to complete it for them. When I taught, I tried to create homework assignments that allowed for family members to be involved, but in an appropriate way. For example, I would ask students to write a paragraph and then ask someone else to read it and tell them whether they had clearly stated the main idea. Or, students would interview a family member or a friend about a topic, and we used the responses in our lessons to provide context or build background.

Ownership

This leads directly to the sixth principle—ownership. Students are more likely to feel as though they have a stake in the assignment if it has some direct link to their lives. It's helpful to provide choices and even ask students to help you choose specific homework options. We've already discussed how to include choices in instruction in Chapter C, "Choices Add Interest." Many of those activities also apply to homework.

Feedback

It's important to provide some type of feedback on homework assignments. This may not be a formal grade; sometimes informal feedback is far more effective. Usually, it's not practical to grade every single activity that your students complete. But students need the opportunity to share and receive feedback on work they have completed, even if it is by sharing their answers with a partner or a small group.

Kid Friendly

All of these characteristics add up to kid-friendly homework. Although the exact format of your homework may depend the age and skill level of each student, generally, effective homework is practical, doable, and interesting.

> **Think About It**
>
> Think about the last activity you assigned for homework. Would you want to do that tonight?

Sample Homework Activities

One of my favorite homework activities comes from an elementary school teacher. She wanted to encourage independent reading with her first graders, so she created reading kits. She found several plastic lunch boxes and transformed each one into a reading project. Inside each box, she placed a book and an activity card. If any supplies were needed (including paper, crayons, or a pencil), she included them in the box. Students were able to take the lunch box home over the weekend to read the book and complete the activity. As she explains, "I never had a problem getting the materials back. My students loved taking the boxes home; they saw it as a treat. And they always completed the activities."

Another teacher in one of my workshops said that she asked her students to bring to class a list of 10 items found in their kitchen at home. Along with the list, students wrote the size of the item and whether it was a quart, a gallon, 16 ounces, a pound, etc. She used this as a springboard for a unit on measurement.

I've talked to teachers at all grade levels who assign homework on the subject of weather. Many teachers work with students to keep a weather log. In kindergarten, this may be as simple as putting a picture on the class calendar of sun, rain, snow, or clouds. By high school, students are taking complicated measurements, including barometric pressure and wind speed. The daily assignment is a practical application of the material.

Kendra Alston uses interactive homework. "I'll take a picture of something my students did in school. Then, I write 'Ask me what I learned today' at the top of the page. The parents have to write what his or her son or daughter said. This lets me know if the students even remember what happened. I'm also always about getting feedback on my own performance and when the parent writes a reflection on what his or her child is learning, it gives you insight on how well you taught." This type of homework requires students to understand what they did in class well enough to explain it to someone else—a high standard. One student told me that she liked this assignment because "it's homework for my mom, not me!"

Summary

- Students want to know that their homework serves a purpose. Provide them with assignments of authentic value, and communicate that value to them daily.
- Homework will be more productive if students have all the tools they need to be successful.
- Practice quality over quantity in assignments.
- Homework can be given to extend, reinforce, or preview content, but it must be an assignment that students can complete successfully with little to no outside support.
- If students have some ownership over homework, they are more likely to complete it.
- To show students that your assignments are important, give prompt feedback.

If You Would Like More Information…

This site consists of an article that provides answers to many homework questions presented by teachers. http://www.educationworld.com/a_admin/admin/admin432.shtml

This site contains an article that presents ways to help students become motivated to do their homework. http://www.educationworld.com/a_curr/curr255.shtml

The Battle Over Homework: Common Ground for Administrators, Teachers, and Parents by Harris Cooper, Corwin Press.

Classroom Instruction That Works: Research-Based Strategies for Increasing Student Achievement by Robert Marzano, Debra Pickering, and Jane Pollock, Association for Supervision and Curriculum Development.

P

Perspective and Points of View

We think too small. Like the frog at the bottom of the well. He thinks the sky is only as big as the top of the well. If he surfaced, he would have an entirely different view.

Mao Tse-tung

One of my challenges as a teacher was to help my students see things from different perspectives. We all have tunnel vision sometimes, making decisions based on our own limited perspective. I believed it was important to provide opportunities for my students to think about a topic from a variety of perspectives. This could be as simple as asking them to read a sentence aloud, pretending to be a different character. For example, saying, "I'm hungry. What's for dinner?" would sound differently if said by a grandmother, a small child, a puppy, or a lion.

Comparing Viewpoints

One of my favorite activities is to compare how different people would view a situation. For example, in a science lesson on pharmaceutical research, you have the perspectives of the researcher who is trying to create a drug that will cure a deadly illness, drug company executives who are considering the profit margin, and patients who are ill and in need of a cure. Use a triangle or another shape that matches the number of sides or perspectives that you want to consider as a visual organizer and write down how each person would view the issue or topic. Students can discuss the different points of view, even creating sample comments for each person, which adds depth to your classroom discussion.

Points of View

Topic	View 1	View 2	View 3
Lunch menu	Cafeteria workers	Student who loves junk food	Student who wants to eat healthy food
Discovery of the New World	Christopher Columbus	Native Americans	King of Spain
Solar system	Copernicus	Contemporaries of Copernicus	Sun
Musical score	Conductor	Musicians	Audience Member
Art	Sculptor or painter	Piece of art	Person looking at art
Word problems in math	The missing number or variable	The solution	The student trying to solve the problem

Two-Voice Poems

Poetry allows students to show creatively that they understand different perspectives. Recently, I was doing a workshop for education majors in which I walked them through the process just described. However, we started with only two perspectives. After drafting the examples, I asked them to write some sample comments that each person or perspective might say. Then, they turned that into a poem of two voices. They wrote the comments as a back-and-forth conversation. Before you decide this is only a language arts activity, look at the examples. Ben Lovelace, a future physical education teacher, developed one to demonstrate the different roles of two basketball players.

Point Guard	Defender
I'm the star of the show.	*I can steal it you know.*
I'm the leader of the pack.	*I'm the one to keep you back.*
I'll let my shots fall like rain.	*I'm the one who wins the games.*
I can take you to the basket with my muscle.	*I'll beat you there with my hustle.*

Laura Husser, a dance major, chose to create a poem to clarify the positions of a dancer's feet. She finishes with a nice twist.

Parallel	Turned Out
I am used mainly in modern.	*I am used mainly in ballet.*
I am a more natural stance.	*I help you move quicker from side to side.*
I activate your abductors.	*I activate your swimsuit muscles.*

By using us both, you get a well-rounded leg.

Debates

Lindsay Yearta uses debates to teach her students to see different perspectives on an issue. She begins with a handout that includes a statement: "I am for/against (insert your topic here)." Next, she assigns each child a position (for or against). The students circle their position on a handout and then research three reasons to support their position. She says, "They get into their groups and come up with what they think the other group would say. What do you think their points are going to be? Then, they write down at least three points their opposition might have and they research comebacks to the opposition's points. So, they have to think ahead and research not only their position, but the other side as well. Then, when we hold our debate, each student had to speak at least once." The verbal exchange is supported by the depth of research on both points of view.

RAFT Strategy

Perhaps you would like your students to write a paragraph about the solar system (the topic you have been teaching in class). This is a standard, lower-level assignment that requires students to restate or summarize the information that you have covered. We can increase the rigor and teach point of view using the RAFT strategy (Santa, Havens, & Macumber, 1996). RAFT stands for *role, audience, format,* and *topic.* Using this strategy, students assume a role, such as an astronaut, and write from that perspective to a more authentic audience, such as a people who read his online blog. In this case, students are required to understand the topic at a higher level in order to complete the task.

RAFT Examples

Role	Audience	Format	Topic
Carrot	Other vegetables	Map	Trip through the digestive system
Chef	Studio audience for cooking show	Script	Recipe
Punctuation mark	Students	Complaint letter	How it is used incorrectly
Water drop	New water drops	Travel guide	Water cycle
Basketball	Alien from another planet	Instructions	How to play the game
Color	Artist	Persuasive letter	Usefulness of a particular color in painting
Penny	Director of the U.S. Mint, the public	Commercial	Request to retire

Missy Miles uses this strategy. "When teaching students to look at things from multiple perspectives, I often start with a RAFT activity. I ask the students to write a letter to their parents asking them to consider bending a rule (extending curfew, letting them go to the mall on the weekends with friends, etc…). Then, I have them reply to the their own letter, this time playing the role of their parent. They have to think of a realistic reply they might get from their parent and include at least two logical reasons for either granting their wish or denying their request. Students have a very hard time doing this at first. I also take controversial issues that really involve them and ask them to do the same thing."

"For example, I may ask them to brainstorm the pros and cons of wearing school uniforms. Most students begin adamantly with the cons list; but I require that their lists be equally long (or short). So, for every con, they are forced to come up with an advantage. I repeatedly have students tell me that they never realized how many arguments there are for the other side. I usually culminate this mini-unit with a research project. They have to choose another controversial issue and research both sides—no matter how biased they are going into it. Then, they must write a persuasive paper arguing for the side they didn't originally favor. I say originally because, once again, I have many students who tell me that the process made them change their minds completely. When I get these comments, I know they have learned how to look at different perspectives of an issue!"

Changing Perspectives in Stories

Many primary and elementary school teachers read a book to their students and then have the class rewrite the book together. After reading *Clifford the Big Red Dog,* for example, students might write about *Margaret, the Small Green Fish.* Another alternative is to have students write a different ending to a book or story they have read. Nancy Anne Kimbel, a fifth-grade teacher at Battleground Elementary School, uses the strategy with her inclusion class, which includes emergent readers, English as a second language students, and dyslexic students. She read the book *Drive-By* by Lynn Ewing with her class. Afterward, she asked her students to write a different ending to the story. Because she had chosen a book that was tailored to her students' interests and then allowed her students to choose their own endings, they were engaged in the lesson and motivated to read more—always a bonus.

Helping your students view the information you are teaching from different perspectives does not have to be difficult or time consuming. You can integrate these simple activities into any content area and, in the process, increase your students' level of engagement.

Summary

- Teach your students to think about life from a variety of perspectives.
- Allow time in class for your students to discuss different viewpoints; it will broaden their horizons. This can happen through informal discussions, writing, or rehearsed debates.
- Looking at issues through different lenses is a life skill. Find ways to include opportunities for students to look at bias and point of view in your classroom, no matter what subject you teach.

If You Would Like More Information...

This site contains information on the use of RAFT and gives examples for the different content areas. http://www.tantasqua.org/Superintendent/Profdevelopment/etraft.html

This site provides student samples involving the use of RAFT. http://www.u-46.org/roadmap/dyncat.cfm?catid=309

Fractured Fairy Tales by A. J. Jacobs, Bantam.

Cinderella Outgrows The Glass Slipper and Other Zany Fractured Fairy Tale Plays by Joan Wolf, Scholastic.

Q

Questioning Strategies

The test of a good teacher is not how many questions he can ask his pupils that they will answer readily, but how many questions he inspires them to ask him which he finds it hard to answer.

Alice Wellington Rollins

Think About It

How often do your students volunteer to answer questions in your class?

Asking and answering questions is an everyday occurrence in most classrooms. Sometimes it happens orally, sometimes in writing, but it is one of the most common classroom activities. Good questioning helps students build understanding, but poor questioning can deter students from learning. How can you create questions that will help all students learn? There are nine key characteristics of good questioning that will help you maximize the use of questions in your lessons.

Characteristics of Good QUESTIONS

Q	Quality
U	Understanding
E	Encourage multiple responses
S	Spark new questions
T	Thought provoking
I	Individualized
O	Ownership shifted to students
N	Narrow and broad
S	Success building

Quality

First, questions should be of high quality. That means each question should be relevant and understandable to your students. Recently, I was in a classroom in which the students were struggling to answer the questions. The teacher assumed they didn't know the content. That wasn't true; they didn't know what he was asking. The questions were very broad and somewhat related to the lesson, but even I wasn't sure what he was asking. The next day, he reviewed the material with a set of clear, focused questions, and the students were more successful.

Understanding

Good questioning serves as a road map for students; it guides them to higher levels of understanding. Barbara Liebhaber of Moravian College in Chicago models a discussion lesson for prospective teachers using guided questioning. Later in the semester, as her students are creating their own lessons, "They discover that asking questions helps their lessons because then the learner owns the information, is more connected to it, finds it relevant and is therefore motivated to learn. When I ask them how they discovered this, they refer back to the lesson that I did on defining the adolescent and see that I was, in fact, modeling that lesson for them. It takes them a while to discover this, but when they do we all get a laugh out of it. They didn't know, at the time, that I was modeling and making the point about questioning students. They thought they were just talking about being teenagers again. In this way, learning is taking place in an active way that is relevant and meaningful for the students. The point is made by modeling and questioning, not telling anything. And it is made in a stronger way than if I told them to ask questions of their students because it is a good way to teach."

Encourage Multiple Responses

As you create questions for your students, remember to build in questions that are open ended, those that have more than one answer. Although it is important to ask questions about facts and details that have only one answer, higher-level questions generally have several possible responses. These "how" and "why" questions will prepare students for life after school.

> **Think About It**
>
> How often are you asked to answer fill-in-the-blank questions?

Spark New Questions

Similarly, good questioning should encourage more questions. In a lesson about food groups, for example, questions about healthy eating might lead your students to ask about the food served for lunch in the cafeteria and the sale of soft drinks in school vending machines. This could lead to a discussion about the school's role in promoting healthy eating. That's exactly what you want to happen. If your students begin to make those connections, it is an indication that they are learning.

Thought Provoking

In addition to prompting new questions, good questioning should provoke students to think. This is more than a regurgitation of facts; it means that students are actively thinking about their learning—what it means, how they are processing the information, and how it connects to their lives. In her book *Yellow Brick Roads: Shared and Guided Paths to Independent Reading 4–12,* Janet Allen (2004) provides categories of questions that allow students to process the content and their own learning. I've adapted it into a bookmark that students can use as they read to prompt questioning. You can do the same thing using categories that are appropriate for your content area.

Questioning Bookmark

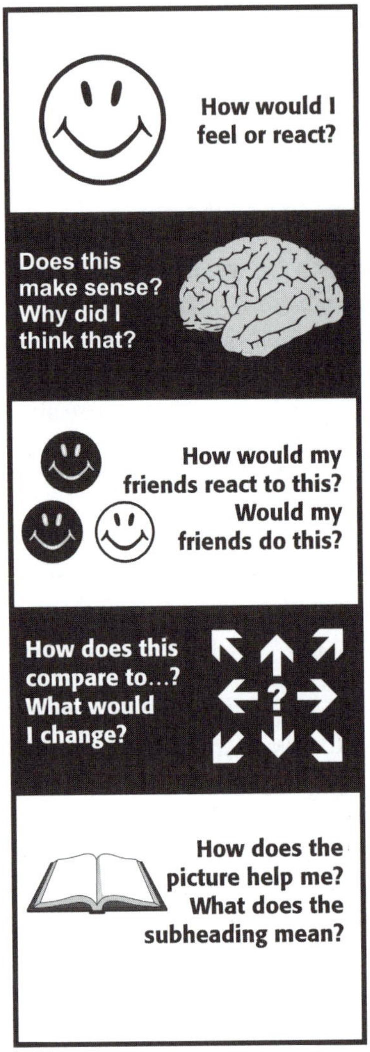
How would I feel or react?
Does this make sense? Why did I think that?
How would my friends react to this? Would my friends do this?
How does this compare to...? What would I change?
?
How does the picture help me? What does the subheading mean?

Individualized

We should also customize questioning techniques for different students. One of my less confident students, Ronnie, was reluctant to volunteer to answer questions. So I would ask him a question that I knew he could answer. Sometimes it was an opinion question rather than a literal, fact-based one. But I wanted to make sure he could be successful so that he would be more confident later. It's also important to provide different ways for students to answer questions.

For example, Cynthia Crump uses "signaling" with her math students. As she explains, "When [my students] are all working individually on a problem, they signal me with their fingers what the answer is. I can stand in the front of the room and acknowledge whether the answer is correct or not very quickly. It beats trying to run around the room and check answers. Plus, the students are very creative in the ways that they present their answers. There is not a 'correct' way. [When] they give me the tens and then the ones for example, sometimes they form the numbers with their fingers, and sometimes they give me the digits, etc. They love it because it moves quickly and allows the slower students to use the time that they need before someone gives the answer out loud. Plus they have immediate feedback. Faster students simply go on the next problem." Her system allows each student to thrive.

Ownership Shifted to Students

Kathy Bumgardner, a former reading specialist for the Gaston County Schools in North Carolina, introduced me to the Question Matrix. This grid crosses basic questions (who, what, when, where, why, and how) with verbs (is, did, can, would, will, and might) to create a matrix that addresses all levels of questioning. If you divide the grid into four quadrants, you'll notice the upper left addresses basic questions; and the closer you get to the bottom right, the higher the level of questioning. I copy the grid on bright colors of card stock, cut the squares apart, and put a complete set in a plastic bag. After my students have read a portion of text or when we are reviewing for a test, I put them into small groups and give each group a bag of cards. In turn, each student draws a card and has to finish the question. For example, if I draw the question "how would," I might ask, "How would you react if you lived in a country that faced a famine?" Then, the rest of the group must answer the question. I've done this with hundreds of teachers, and you can use these questions with almost any topic. It's interactive and engaging, but most important, it shifts ownership of the activity to students. They are responsible for creating their own questions, and that requires them to understand the material at a higher level.

Question Matrix

What Is	When Is	Where Is	Which Is	Who Is	Why Is	How Is
What Did	When Did	Where Did	Which Did	Who Did	Why Did	How Did
What Can	When Can	Where Can	Which Can	Who Can	Why Can	How Can
What Would	When Would	Where Would	Which Would	Who Would	Why Would	How Would
What Will	When Will	Where Will	Which Will	Who Will	Why Will	How Will
What Might	When Might	Where Might	Which Might	Who Might	Why Might	How Might

From Wiederhold, C. (1995). *Cooperative Learning and Higher Level Thinking: The Q-Matrix.* San Clemente, CA: Kagan Publishing.

Narrow and Broad

Earlier, I mentioned the importance of using open-ended, higher-level questioning. There is a balance. Because knowledge is based on facts, you want to include questions that are narrow and focused on a single answer. However, you also want to include questions that are broader and are generally considered application questions. Bloom's taxonomy is a helpful planning tool.

Sample Questions for an Elementary Science Lesson on the Inner Planets Using Bloom's Taxonomy

Remembering:	What is the closest planet to the sun?
Understanding:	Why is a year on Mercury much shorter than a year on Earth?
Applying:	How old would you be if you lived on Mars?
Analyzing:	Why is it possible to live on Earth but not on Mars?
Evaluating:	Do you think we should be spending so much time and effort on space exploration?
Creating:	What would a colony on the moon need to have? (Use your knowledge of the elements needed to sustain life.)

Success Building

Each of the previous recommendations supports the critical purpose of good questioning, leading your students to successful learning. Questions are not simply part of your lesson; they are the key to unlocking understanding for students. Too often, we ask students to read or listen to something and then assume that they know it. Real understanding is more than that, and it doesn't happen through osmosis. It happens when students interact with knowledge in a way that enables them to connect it to what they already know and to their own experiences. Good questioning helps them with that process and ensures their success.

Summary

- When teachers carefully craft their questions, a higher level of understanding is achieved than when all of the questions are spontaneous.
- Construct questions that ask students to think critically and provide support for their answers. Higher-level questions that have more than one right answer require students to stretch their minds.
- Good questions encourage more good questions. They spark a chain of questioning that leads to enhanced learning.
- Differentiate your questions. All students need to feel successful. For some, that means answering simple questions correctly to build confi-

dence. Know the level at which each student needs to be challenged and use that information to customize your questioning.

- Share ownership with your students; let them create questions, too.
- Strike a balance between narrow and broad questions; there are times when each is appropriate.

If You Would Like More Information…

This site includes questioning strategies for teacher and student questions. http://cte.udel.edu/TAbook/question.html

This side contains the new and revised Bloom's taxonomy: http://www.apa.org/ed/new_blooms.html/.

Q Tasks: How to Empower Students to Ask Questions and Care About Answers. By C. Koechlin and S. Zwaan, Pembroke Publishers Limited.

Improving Classroom Questions, Second Edition by Kenneth R. Chuska, Phi Delta Kappa International.

Teaching Question-and-Relationship Revisited by Taffy Raphael, The Reading Teacher.

Classroom Motivation from A to Z, by Barbara R. Blackburn, Eye On Education. (See chapter U).

R

Reflection Adds Depth to Learning

By three methods we may learn wisdom: First, by reflection, which is noblest; Second, by imitation, which is easiest; and Third by experience, which is the bitterest.

Confucius

Do you take time to reflect? If you are like most teachers I know, slowing down enough to think about what you are doing isn't easy given all your responsibilities. But it's important to stop and think about what you are doing. What did you do that was effective? What didn't work as you had planned? How might you change a lesson the next time you teach it? Which students surprised you today—in a positive way? When we take time to reflect, we increase our own learning. The same is true for our students. They need opportunities for deeper learning, and reflection is one of the steps along that path. There are three types of reflection for students: reflecting on what they have learned, reflecting on how they learn, and reflecting on their progress.

Reflecting on What I Have Learned

There are many informal ways to have students reflect on what they have learned. You can do this orally by periodically asking them to turn to a partner and explain what they understand. Or you can ask students to write a classified ad, selling what they learned today in your class. In 25 words or less, students should describe what they learned and the importance of the learning. They can even price its value. Sometimes I use sticky notes, writing a question or prompt on a poster and asking students to respond individually on a sticky note. Then, I can rearrange the notes in categories and use the responses to guide our class discussion.

I've also seen teachers use journals effectively. Students write entries explaining the main idea they learned in the lesson and a question they still have. These serve as a springboard for review or discussion during the next class. Or the journal can be used as a learning log. Every day at the end of class, students write down at least one thing they learned. By the end of the week, they have a list of at least five things they have learned, by the end of the month they have 20, and so on. This is more authentic than a test and allows students to see and personalize what they are learning.

Providing multiple, authentic opportunities for students to think about what they have learned is the key. The actual format doesn't matter. I like to vary what I do, if for no other reason than to prevent boredom.

Reflecting on How I Learn

Most of the reflection opportunities that students have focus on what they have learned. But it's also important for them to think about *how* they are learning. Math teachers Lindsay Grant and Christy Matkovich incorporate opportunities in which students can reflect on their own learning processes. Students are given the opportunity to rework any problems that were incorrect on a test.

As the graphic organizer shows, students are also asked to think about their learning by explaining why they missed the original question and why they know they have the correct answer now. As Lindsay explains, the process "makes them think about what they've done and what they did differently or what they are supposed to do."

Understanding Math Better

Name ____ Date _____________

Math Test ______________ Teacher _________________________________

Question:

My original answer:

My new solution (you must show your work, including all steps):

The correct answer:

Why I missed the question on the original test (circle one):

I didn't understand the question.

I thought I had it right.

I skipped a step.

I studied this but I forgot.

I had no clue about this.

I ran out of time or guessed.

I made a careless mistake.

Why I know I have the right answer now:

A self-assessment checklist can help your students think about how they learn. It can also help you design lessons that will connect with your students. A variety of learning style assessments are available, but simply asking your students to think about what they like to do can provide valuable information. This simple checklist for elementary school students is a good starting point.

Self-Assessment

	Yes	No
I like to learn new things.		
I like to draw.		
I like to read.		
I like to write.		
I like to talk to other people.		
I like to make things.		
I like to wiggle and move around.		

Reflecting on My Progress

Everyone needs an opportunity to reflect on their progress. Without it, we tend to forget that we are making progress! Often, we track the progress of our students through stickers, check marks, or some other form of data collection, but our students need the chance to keep up with their own successes. One way is to have your students keep a Victory List in the back of their journals or student agendas. A Victory List is simply a personal list of successes.

Sample Victory List

I completed the science lab successfully.

I knew the answer when my teacher called on me.

I learned a new strategy for organizing information.

I participated in the volleyball game during physical education.

I used information I learned in math during my job.

The purpose of the Victory List is to help us remember what we have accomplished, particularly when things aren't going so well. Over time, it also builds a track record of success for learning.

You might consider adapting this to a more public presentation. I am often asked, "How should I display examples of my students' work?" It's a challenge because you want to reward good work, but you also don't want to exclude students who may not be perfect. Christy, one of my former graduate students, has found a terrific way to balance the two and shift ownership to her middle school students, all of whom scored below the basic level on their most recent achievement test. She created a Wall of Fame by adding a butterfly border to a bulletin board in her room. Her students pick what they want to post. They can choose a sample of their work or something that they did well, such as answering a question correctly in class. In the latter case, students write what they did on a paper "Pat on the Back" and post it. For each posted item, her students must explain to her why they are proud of the work. That's her only criteria, but the process requires her students to reflect on their progress.

Reflection requires students to take ownership of their learning. And teaching students to reflect can be hard work. But if we truly want students to be independent learners, reflection is one of the key building blocks.

Summary

- We all need to reflect on our experiences; this includes your students. Teaching them to reflect in different ways will help them deepen their learning.
- Reflection can be a very formal process or a quick, informal check.
- Provide multiple, authentic opportunities for your students to think about the way they learn.
- Students benefit from understanding how they learn best. Checklists or learning inventories can help your students think metacognitively.
- Shift ownership to your students by teaching them how to reflect on their own progress.

If You Would Like More Information…

This site provides sample self-assessment charts. http://www.ingilish.com/selfassess.htm

This site provides teachers with links to reflection activities as well as information regarding the benefits of student reflection. http://writing.colostate.edu/guides/teaching/service_learning/reflect.cfm

Student Reflection Journal for Student Success by Susan Landgraf, Prentice Hall.

Teaching, Learning, and Assessment Together: The Reflective Classroom by Arthur Ellis, Eye On Education.

5

Show Them What You Are Thinking

If we don't model what we teach, then we are teaching something else.

Author unknown

> **Think About It**
>
> Do your students become confused in the middle of a lesson?

How often are your students confused? Mine were confused more often that I'd like to remember. Some of your students, particularly your struggling learners, need to understand what is happening in your head. They need you to show them what you think and how you think.

One teacher told me, "Most students turn in their best idea of what we are looking for. Sometimes they really don't know what we are thinking, and it's our job to make sure they do know." There are several ways to model thinking for your students: modeling expected behaviors, thinking aloud, using Guide-o-Ramas, modeling a process, and modeling instructional expectations.

Modeling Expected Instructional Behaviors

You probably have some basic expectations for your students related to instruction. However, your students may not understand what to do, even if you tell them. Tracy Smith, a former language arts teacher, found this to be true. "What [my students] really needed from me was a model. So, I sat in a student desk and did what I wanted the students to do. On the first day, it was a little rocky. They came in socializing like normal adolescents. Then, they would notice me and start asking, 'What is she doing?' Someone inevitably would say, 'Oh, she's writing in her journal. That's what we're supposed to do when we come into this class.' Or 'She's reading a book. I think we're supposed to get our books and begin reading.' After a day or two, it became routine. When we had times for sharing, students always wanted to know what I was writing and reading. The payoff was incredible."

Thinking Aloud

Many students at all grade levels struggle with the organization of textbooks. They may not know that chapter subheadings form an outline or that boldface words are important new terms that are likely defined in the sentence, in the glossary, and possibly even in the margin. It is important to teach your students how to use your specific textbook. One way is simply to talk students through the book. "This year, we're using a new textbook in my class. And one of the things I did was sit down and look through it and see what is available to help me use the textbook most effectively. So for example, you will see a box with words at the beginning of each chapter. Those are important, and they are usually new words, so don't worry if you don't already know what they mean. They are part of the lesson, and there is also a definition in the glossary at the back of the book." Then just walk them through the other key elements in the book.

You can follow the same process with any instruction. The purpose is simple: to show your students how you are processing information. When working with her struggling math students, Christy Matkovich talks through how she solves word problems.

Word Problem Think Aloud

Ms. Mazzeroni raises guppies. One day, she donated 20 of her fish to a local middle school science classroom. She then went out and bought the same number of guppies that were left in her fishbowl at home. She divided the fish equally and sold them to six customers. Each customer bought 15 fish. How many fish did she have to begin with?

Have each student read the word problem silently. Then call on one child to read the problem aloud to everyone.

Teacher: What is it that Ms. Mazzeroni is raising?

Student: Guppies.

Teacher: What are we trying to figure out in this problem?

Student: How many fish she started with.

Teacher: Let's highlight the question so we will remember what we are looking for.

Teacher: Now, I don't know how many fish she started with, but I do know some different things that she did with her fish. Can someone tell me the first thing she did with her guppies?

Student: Donated 20 of them to a middle school.

Teacher: OK, I am going to write that down so I do not forget she gave 20 of them away—or I am going to highlight that because it is an important fact?

Teacher: Then it says she went out and bought the same number of guppies that were still left in her fish bowl. I wonder what that means? Lets say she had 35 fish and gave 20 away, how many fish would be left in her tank?

Student: 15 fish.

Teacher: So if she then went out and bought the same number that were left in her fish bowl, does that mean she went out and bought 15 more fish to give her a total of 30? I am going to write that down [highlight that part in the problem] because that sounds pretty important.

Teacher: The last thing it says she did was equally divide the amount of fish she had to six customers. So this means that the number of fish in the bowl has to be divisible by six. Can anyone give me some numbers that are divisible by 6?

Student: 6, 12, 18, 24, …

Teacher: Now wait a minute—If I keep reading, it says each customer receives 15 fish. So if she gives six customers 15 fish a piece, how many fish did she divide?

Student: You would have to multiply, 6 times 15.

Teacher:	Excellent thought! So if I multiply 6 by 15, that means she gave out 90 fish. [Do the work on the board talking through the multiplication process.] Now I know she didn't start with 90 because I have some other facts highlighted in my problem that I need to go back and look at. If she gave out 90 after she bought some more, how many did she have before she bought the extra guppies? Well, I know that she bought the same amount as were in her tank—which is the same as doubling or multiplying times two. It seems like I am working backward on this problem. Therefore, if I know she doubled the amount in her tank, and I need to work backward to see how many she started with, what operation would I need to do?
Student:	The opposite of multiplying is dividing.
Teacher:	Wonderful! So if she gave out 90, and she had half of that before she bought some, how many did she have in the tank? Well, 90 divided by 2 is… [Talk through the division problem as you work it on the board.]
Student:	45 guppies.
Teacher:	Now, I know she had 45 guppies in her tank before she bought any extra fish. However, I know I am not finished because I still have an important fact I highlighted that I have not used yet. What is that fact?
Student:	She gave 20 away to a middle school.
Teacher:	Exactly! Now, again I am working backward to see how many fish she started with. So right now I know she had 45 before she bought any extra fish. I wonder how many she had before she gave away the first 20. Do I subtract 20 or add 20? Well, if I am working backward, and I want to know how many she had *before* she did anything with her fish, I would probably… [Pause for awhile thinking, giving the students time to think. Someone will raise a hand.]
Student:	You would have to add the 20 fish.
Teacher:	Excellent problem solving! So I would have to add 20 fish to the 45 fish, and I would come up with 65 fish that she started with. Before we move on, let's see whether 65 fish makes sense. [Then work through the problem forward, using the 65 fish, and following everything Ms. Mazzeroni does to see whether you come back to giving six customers 15 fish apiece.]

See how simple it is? In fact, it's so automatic for us, we assume everyone else would know how to think through that process. Your strong students will be able to do that in their heads, but your struggling students will not understand. That's why it's important to model your thinking for students.

Using Guide-O-Ramas

Ideally, you would have time to individually work with every student who is struggling in your classroom and guide them through the content. Unfortunately, that's not possible all the time. One alternative is to guide them in writing using a Guide-o-Rama. You may already give your students a study guide or a set of questions to follow as they read a selection. The Guide-o-Rama intersperses a written think-aloud into the process. This is a helpful alternative when you want to support individual students or when you want students to work on their own.

Guide-O-Rama Study Guides

Europe: War and Change—Chapter 12 (Sections 12.1–12.2)

Page	Reading Tip
326	Look at the map. This gives you an idea of where Europe is in relation to the United States.
327	Read the introduction in the yellow box. Can you believe that most Europeans can speak at least three languages? Can you speak any languages other than English?
329–332	Read section 12.1. Pay close attention to the terms *nationalism, colonialism,* and *dual monarchy.* They are related and can be confusing!
334–338	As you read this section carefully, make a timeline of which countries joined the war and record the dates when each joined.
335	I found it interesting that dogs were used in the war to detect mines and guard ammunition! Do you think this is humane?
336	Pay close attention to the term *fascism.* How does this compare to what you know about communism and democracy?

Modeling a Process

Jessica Neuberger uses modeling to prepare social studies students for their first student-led portfolio assessment conferences. As she explains, "I taped a sample interview to give the students a good idea of what to expect. When the class viewed the sample interview, I would stop the video after each question, have the students repeat each question to me and then they would write it down. The second time through, we watched the whole interview with no interruptions. Then we discussed it. When I interviewed the students throughout the next week, they were prepared to share their work with me, offer me their opinions of their strengths and weaknesses, and we were able to set a goal for the next part of the year." Because she knew this would be challenging for her students, she modeled the entire process for them and then provided scaffolded instruction to ensure their success.

Modeling Instructional Expectations

Many students do not understand our expectations for a product. As we discussed in Chapter N, "Next Steps," we often ask students to complete an assignment, and we are frustrated when the quality of work does not match our expectations. Some students don't know what to do or how to do it, and some may think that what they are doing is right. Therefore, it's important to define what you are looking for, explain it to your students, and show them examples.

Jill Yates follows this process in her art instruction. "The most effective modeling that I have found has been in my use of example and nonexample. Especially when I use this technique in art, the visible and concrete examples that are set before the students really help solidify what a desired and appropriate end product might look like. This is not to suggest that any of our products lack originality or creativity. Each is always unique. What I have found is that in the process of comparing two samples (an example and nonexample) and discussing and comparing the qualities of each, there remains no mystery in what is considered high quality and complete as a class. I tend to use my own stories and experiences, plus student examples, to add high drama and humor within the task of comparing. I often start the year by comparing products extremely dissimilar in nature, and end the year comparing more subtle and/or equal products simply to encourage analysis, discussion, and higher level thinking. I have found that in using examples and nonexamples not only are standards met with more confidence, but rubrics are also created most naturally and quickly."

It takes extra time to build modeling into your instruction, but the results are worth the effort. As Jill says, "Modeling is my absolute favorite part of any lesson, especially at the introductory level. I have learned that in allowing myself to be vulnerable by using my own examples, experiences, and sense of confusion, it has offered the most powerful learning for both myself and my students."

Summary

- Be a model. Your students need to see how you think and how you complete certain tasks.
- Students are watching every move you make; nothing goes unnoticed.
- If you want a student to read, model reading; if you want a student to paint, model painting. In short, show them what you want them to do.
- When it's impossible to model your thought process aloud, try writing it down for students to read.
- Give an example of what good work looks like. We all want to know what is expected of us before we begin a task.

If You Would Like More Information...

This site contains an article that shows teachers how to model the think-aloud method of reading comprehension to their students and how to show students to reflect on their work. http://www.indiana.edu/~crls/rogerfarr/mcr/usingta/usingta.html

This site contains an article on how to incorporate daily math skills through problem solving. http://content.scholastic.com/browse/article.jsp?id=3584

This site provides a list of resources teachers can use for using the think-aloud method in the different content areas. http://www.literacymatters.org/content/study/think.htm

Improving Comprehension with Think-Alouds: Modeling What Good Readers Do. By Jeffrey Wilhelm, Scholastic.

T

Turn the Tables: Helping Students Take Responsibility for Their Own Learning

The greatest gifts you can give your children are the roots of responsibility and the wings of independence.

Denis Waitley

I was talking with a teacher about the structured approach for supporting students that we discussed in Chapter N, "Next Steps." She said, "That's doing all the work for them. It's not real life. Students need to learn to take responsibility!" I agreed but reminded her that students need structure and support in order to be successful, particularly when it comes to new and challenging work. Then we need to teach them to take responsibility for their own learning rather than look to us for the answers. Balancing the two is a life skill. An engineer compared it to the difference between tactical and strategic planning. If you are engaged in tactical planning, you are typically provided step-by-step details to follow. Some jobs require that skill, and that's what we discussed in the Next Steps chapter.

However, some jobs require strategic planning, which means that you may be given a desired end result, but you have flexibility in how you move toward that result. That's the purpose of this chapter: to give you suggestions for moving your students toward learning that require them to be more independent. As you give your students choices and opportunities for leadership, you'll also build their ownership in learning.

Responsibility Through Goal Setting

One of the most effective ways to help students take responsibility for their learning is through goal setting. As the Success Cycle shows, when students set goals and achieve those goals, they build self-confidence and become more willing to try again.

This can be as simple as asking students to list what they want to learn in a specific lesson, or it can be more complex. For example, Tracy Smith incorporates goal setting into her language arts classes. Her students "make decisions about their own learning goals and grades. They know up front what is required for an A, B, and C. They develop their own plans for achieving. Almost all of the students begin with a goal of A. Even when they do not meet their goal, they typically do better than they had in past classes when all assignments were teacher-driven and directed."

Success Cycle

Responsibility in Learning Activities

Another way to teach students responsibility is to give them choices in learning activities. Jill Yates uses a workshop approach with her first graders. "Academically speaking, I have found that choices are very motivating and important in validating students' interests and abilities. My partner and I try very hard to include different workshop times within our day. You can imagine that in first grade, workshop looks different at different points within our year, but we work with our class to understand that having choices and being accountable to work are not wholly separate. As we release more workshop responsibility into their hands, we create systems to coach this understanding. After establishing the atmosphere and rules of workshop, we allow students to begin to choose the order in which they would like to complete their tasks. Sometimes we create a 'have to' job first, when something has high priority, but we often allow the students to decide the order in which they would like to approach the items. As we help monitor and manage time, students progress through the centers or activities and mark their names off of designated lists as each activity is completed. At the end of the workshop session, we can glance over the lists to see whose names are still visible (or not crossed off). For students who need a more structured approach to help manage their time, we help plan an order with them, and coach them through the process with plenty of check-in and fly-by observations."

Chris Webb takes a different approach with his eighth-grade social studies students. After teaching a unit on the U.S. Constitution, the Bill of Rights, and the American Revolution, his students must create a culminating project to demonstrate their understanding of the concepts. Each student creates a book titled *How to Create a Free Country.* As Webb explains, "Though they must follow some standard requirements, they have the freedom to make any type of how-to format. It can be written like an instruction manual or a cookbook, etc." A clear rubric ensures that his students know the basic guidelines.

His balance of providing set requirements with choices not only increases involvement and builds a sense of ownership and pride with his students but also requires students to demonstrate a high level of understanding.

Responsibility in Assessment

Another way to shift responsibility for learning is through the use of contracts. Developing a plan that is an agreement among the teacher, student, and family members can support student learning. I've seen this done informally. For example, in one class, students write letters about what they want to accomplish during the school year. The teacher then writes a letter responding and supporting the students' goals and detailing how she will assist each student. Both are sent home, and a parent or family member writes a third letter agreeing to the goals and explaining how he or she will help. Copies of all three letters are given to the student, family, and teacher. During a conference at the end of the year, the teacher, student, and parents discuss whether the student achieved his or her goals and outline next steps. One parent commented, "I felt like I was part of the team. And I was glad to agree to help." In this approach, the teacher shares ownership of learning and moves the assessment discussion further than grades or a test score.

Some teachers use learning contracts for grades (see the sample in Chapter J). Using this approach, the teacher prepares a list of assignments or projects that relate to the objectives in a particular unit. Points are assigned to each item, and a description of the points necessary to achieve each grade is provided, along with a time frame for completion. Students choose the projects they would like to do based on the point values and the grade they would like to achieve. Contracts can help build student ownership; however, make sure you have clear guidelines and expectations. You may need to provide additional support to students who are less self-directed.

Transitioning to Ownership

Helping students take ownership of their learning is important. One day you won't be there, and your students need to be independent. But you can't just give your students work and leave them alone. You need to structure opportunities that allow them to take ownership and then teach them how to grow. As Jill Yates reminds us, "I learned early on that I had to make no assumptions in believing that my students naturally knew what was expected, how to transition, and what being accountable and responsible for good choices meant. I have come to realize that my explicit consistency and modeling are what create and sustain the strong foundational and operational understanding I seek. And, I have found this in turn creates classes that desire and choose to pursue success, confidence, and pride."

Summary

- There are times when students need step-by-step instruction and assistance; however, other learning situations lend themselves to opportunities for student ownership. You must carefully decide when each is appropriate.

- By teaching students goal-setting strategies, you are working to increase their sense of responsibility.
- Giving students simple choices throughout the instructional process can help develop a sense of ownership.
- When gradually giving students responsibility, clear guidelines and expectations are crucial for success.
- The picture of a responsible student is confidence and pride.

If You Would Like More Information...

Self-Efficacy: Raising the Bar for All Students (2nd Edition) by Joanne Eisenberger, Marcia Conti-D'Antonio, & Robert Bertrando, Eye on Education.

*Goal Setting for Success: Handbook for Teachers,*by Jerry Rottier, National Middle School Association.

This site provides teachers with links to different strategies for helping students to take responsibility for their own learning. http://www.mvrhs.org/eel/caruthers/linkforallteachers/index.html

On Equal Terms: How to Make the Most of Learning Contracts in Grades 4-9 by Scott Greenwood, Heinemann.

Classroom Motivation from A to Z, by Barbara R. Blackburn, Eye On Education. (See chapters G and O).

U

Understand Your Audience

You can't teach what you don't understand.

Susan Kovalik

> **Think About It**
>
> Do you teach students or subject matter?

During one of my workshops on student motivation, a gentleman asked me, "How quickly can you tell me everything I need to know about how to motivate my students?" He was surprised at my response. I said, "That's simple, I can tell you everything you need to know in 10 seconds. In order to motivate your students, you need to care about them, and you need to connect with them." He sat back down, and then I continued. "But the hard part is the connecting. Almost everyone I meet cares about students. The most effective teachers I know connect with their students in very specific ways."

In this chapter, we'll talk about the foundation of caring and connecting—understanding your students. You can't really care about them or connect with them if you don't know who they are. One of your most important tasks should be learning everything you can about your students. You probably have some formal information about them (test scores, interest inventories, etc.), but we're going to look at other ways to learn about your students from the best possible source, your students themselves. Each of the activities in this chapter will help you understand who they are, their thoughts, feelings, struggles, goals, and dreams.

Culture Boxes

A creative way to learn about your students is through the use of Culture Boxes. At the beginning of the year, ask your students to put 7–10 items that represent different aspects of who they are into a shoebox. Your students will love this activity, so visit your local shoe store and get lots of shoe boxes of varying sizes. You'l! have at least one student who needs the large, boot-sized box. As Charlesetta Dawson explains, "These objects reflect their family heritage, origins, ethnicity, language, religion, hobbies, and likes (foods, music, literature, movies, sports, etc.). The outsides of the boxes are decorated with pictures, symbols, and words/phrases to further explain who they are. Then the students share their culture boxes with the class. Every semester, my students always say that creating a culture box was their favorite activity because they got to be creative, share previously unknown information about themselves with their peers and teacher, and develop a better understanding of the similarities that we all have in common. The sharing might take more than one class period, but the time spent is well worth it!"

Venn Diagrams

One of my favorite activities is to create a physical Venn diagram using two jump ropes on the floor. I pick a student to stand inside one circle, then another to stand inside the second circle. I ask the other students to guess what criteria I'm using to sort the students. I continue to ask students to stand in one circle or the other or in the overlap between the two if the person fits in both categories until they guess my criteria. I start with something simple, such as color of clothing or type of shoes. Then I use characteristics that aren't as visual, such as common interests.

Next, I let my students continue the game, sorting people based on what they have learned about each other. Because I give bonus points for coming up with criteria that are different and harder to guess, the students learn things that their classmates have in common. I was recently in a primary school classroom where the class had completed a similar activity; however, the students then made posters of a Venn diagram comparing themselves and a classmate. The interaction shifts ownership of learning to students, and you learn a tremendous amount about your students in the process.

Creating Timelines

Another option is to ask students to create a timeline of their experiences. Students can include when they were born, years they were in certain grade levels, the birth of siblings, and other typical experiences. They can also highlight unusual experiences they have had, such as going to band camp, traveling, learning a new skill, and so on. Create a class timeline to showcase students' common experiences. Next, add photos (take digital pictures and print them) and post your class timeline on the wall. You can also put the individual timelines into a notebook to create a class book. This becomes a terrific tool to help parents, administrators, and substitute teachers learn about your students.

Writing Autobiographies

If you prefer, you can ask students to write their autobiographies. Sarah Ehrman explains, "My first assignment is [to ask students to write an] autobiography. Everyone wants a chance to tell their story—where they were born, about their family. They write about a sport, extracurricular activities, anything they want. They are motivated when they think you want to know about them. When I started my first job, it was because the other teacher quit. They had had 15 subs before I came, and they knew they were 'bad kids.' One of the students told other teachers [they] were so surprised that I cared enough to have them write three pages and that I cared enough to read it."

Writing accomplishes two purposes. First, you learn about your students. Second, they learn that you care about them. By the way, creating the timeline first helps your students organize their thoughts for the autobiography.

Writing Vision Letters

In *Classroom Motivation From A to Z,* I recommend that teachers write vision letters. The task is to imagine that it is the last day of school. Write a letter or e-mail message to another teacher describing your year: all that your students have accomplished, how they have changed, and what they have learned from you. I find that writing the letter helps define your purpose and set your priorities. During my workshops, we do this activity and then discuss what our visions mean in terms of instruction. This is also a good activity to do with students. When you ask your students to write a letter explaining why this was the best year of their lives, it helps you learn about them. Chris Webb, one of my graduate students, opens his school year with this activity.

"With the letters, I wrote on the board for the kids to write why they had had the most successful year in Mr. Webb's social studies class. This was the second day of school, and all I had talked to them about were my rules and school rules—I had not yet done any introduction activities. I told them they only needed to write a short paragraph, not a novel, but most wrote a half page, some wrote more. Some of the things they wrote about were not getting into any trouble, how they had gotten into trouble and had gotten bad grades in sixth and seventh grade and that did not happen this year, etc. It was a great activity because I got to know my students early on, and I think the kids really appreciated starting off on the right foot. Sort of like Harry Wong says, this is one of those early activities that will determine the type of year I will have. So far so good. I plan on keeping their letters in a file, and if students start to slip up with grades or behavior, I can pull the letter out and talk to them about it before there is a negative consequence."

Just after he told me about his experiences, I was at St. Paul Primary School. I spotted two bulletin boards on which the teachers, Evelyn Shuler and Nancy Tindal, had posted second graders' vision letters. I was amazed to read the comments: "I learned how to read a chapter book." "I learned how to subtract." "I learned how to spell words like September." And my personal favorite, "I learned how to be good and not pull sticks." (Pulling popsicle sticks is part of the discipline plan.) I was struck by the young students' focus and their understanding of the importance of learning and good behavior. Vision letters can help you tap into students' goals and priorities, which you can then use in your instruction.

There are so many ways that you can learn about your students—the key is simply to do it! The more you understand who they are and how they think, the better you will be at responding to their needs through your instruction. And when you connect with them on a personal level, they will be more responsive to you, and their learning will increase.

Summary

- Know your students. Make connections with them that go beyond academics. Take a genuine interest in their lives; you'll be able to reach them more effectively.
- Celebrate diversity. Allow students to share their culture and family heritage. Not only will your classes grow closer, you'll gain insight into the background knowledge of each student.
- Create opportunities for students to learn about one another. The class atmosphere can change dramatically when you establish an environment of respect, appreciation of differences, and empathy.

If You Would Like More Information...

This site provides a variety of icebreakers and other activities you can use to get to know your students. http://www.teachervision.fen.com/students/relationships/2878.html

This site provides links to various inclusive strategies for teachers to get to know their students. http://depts.washington.edu/cidrweb/inclusive/students.html

Understanding Your Child's Temperament. by William B. Carey, Martha Moraghan Jablow, and the Children's Hospital of Philadelphia. Macmillan.

V

Victory with Vocabulary

"I never knew words could be so confusing," Milo said to Tock as he bent down to scratch the dog's ear. "Only when you use a lot to say a little," answered Tock. Milo thought this was quite the wisest thing he'd heard all day.—

Norman Juster, *The Phantom Tollbooth*

Think About It

Do your students really learn new vocabulary terms, or do they memorize them for a test?

How many of your students struggle to understand new vocabulary terms? My students did, particularly in social studies. It's especially difficult to understand the specialized vocabulary found in content-area courses. Words that may seem familiar have a different meaning in the new context. For example, I was in a science classroom, and Eric was sure he knew the definition of the term *grounded.* As he explained that he was grounded for two weeks because of a low grade on a test, the other students laughed. The teacher was looking for an answer about the grounding of electricity, which is quite different. However, it provided an important lesson for the students and for us about the ease with which words can be confusing.

If you want your students to successfully learn your content, you will reap dividends if you invest time in teaching vocabulary. When I was a student, the model for teaching vocabulary was pretty simple. The teacher gave the class a list of words, we copied the words and definitions, and then we wrote a sentence using each term. Finally, we took a test. Sadly, that's still the model used in many classrooms. That is like an upside-down V—a pointed introduction and the assumption that students will build a broad base of knowledge and understanding.

There is a more effective way to teach vocabulary; simply turn the V right-side up. Start by designing your instruction to give students a wide range of experiences with words used in context, connect the new information with what your students already know, and provide opportunities for them to play with words so that they will leave your classroom with an understanding that is exactly on point.

Models for Teaching Vocabulary

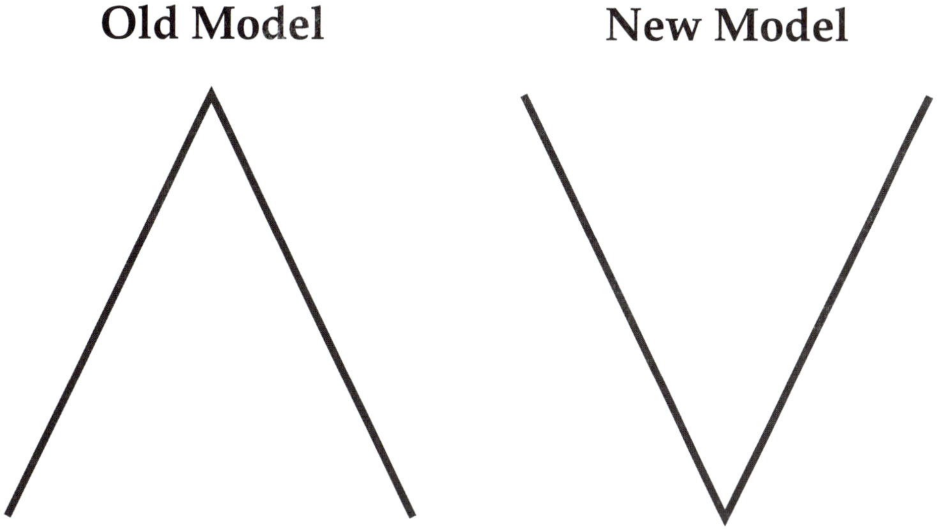

Introducing New Words

Some teachers prefer to preteach vocabulary terms before a lesson; others find it more effective to provide instruction during the lesson as students experience the new words. I've used both methods, and I have a basic rule: Do what works for the students, but provide instruction throughout the lesson. Direct instruction is important; students will not learn new words through osmosis.

As I plan my lessons, I try to predict whether my students will view a new vocabulary word as a bump in the road or as a wall that stops learning. If it is a major concept and I think it will be a wall, then I teach it before the lesson using a graphic organizer (see Chapter G for examples).

Checking Prior Knowledge

You may not be sure whether your students understand an important term, so it's important to find out what your students already know. Pat Vining, a high school math teacher, uses a simple activity to check her students' prior knowledge of the concept and to clear up any misunderstandings students may have about the topic. First, she gives students three minutes to answer a short true/false questionnaire. Next, in pairs, students compare responses and use the textbook to check their answers. Each set of partners must rewrite any false statements so that they are true. She ends with a whole-class discussion to ensure understanding.

Pythagorean Theorem

Directions: Check whether the statement is true or false.

____ 1. The longest side of a triangle is called the hypotenuse.

____ 2. In the Pythagorean theorem, the variable c stands for the hypotenuse.

____ 3. Any side in a right triangle is called a leg.

____ 4. A corollary is a statement that can be easily proved using a theorem.

____ 5. If you know the lengths of all three sides of a right triangle, you can use the Pythagorean theorem to determine whether it is a right triangle.

Using Visuals to Enhance Understanding

Visuals can help students understand new concepts. I was in a social studies classroom in which the teacher was presenting geography terms such as *equator, latitude,* and *longitude.* She drew a circle on the board to illustrate the Earth, and then she wrote the word *equator* across the center. She wrote the word *latitude* horizontally from west to east where the latitude lines go across the Earth. Finally, she wrote the word *longitude* from north to south to clearly illustrate the meaning of the word. She provided visual context for her students as they encountered the terms for the first time.

Equator

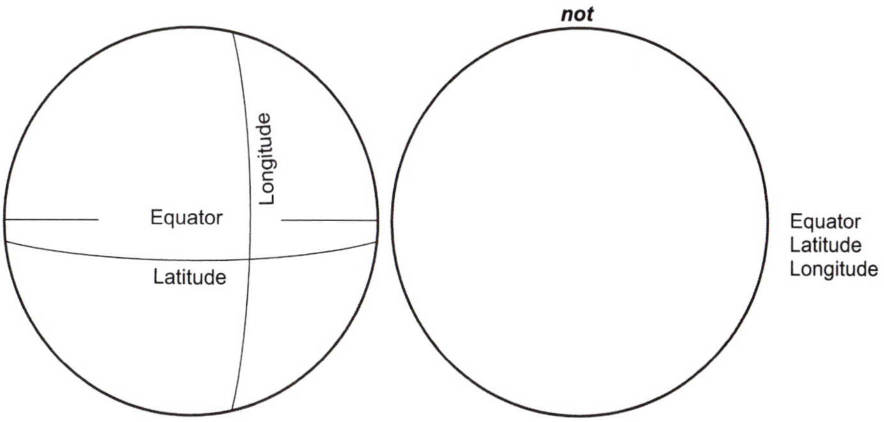

Erin Owens, a first-grade teacher, uses a visual game to provide context for new words. During "Three Alike," she writes three words on the board or overhead projector. Students then have to explain what the words have in common. This is a terrific way to help your class connect a new word to words they already know. You can categorize words in a variety of ways depending on your purpose (parts of speech, common characteristics, beginning sounds, number of letters). As an extension, you can ask students to add other words to your list.

Playing Games

We need to experience new words and concepts multiple times in a variety of ways. Too often, we expect students to fully understand a word after they have read it one time. However, reading a word multiple times doesn't ensure understanding either. Your students need to play with words in fun and different ways to help them learn.

During "Head Band," Erin writes a word on a sentence strip and makes it into a headband. First graders in her class give clues to the person wearing the headband, who must guess the word. All students are involved, and the activity encourages her students to learn from each other.

James Good, a middle school drama teacher, points out that his students find the language of Shakespearean plays challenging. For key scenes, students are broken into groups with five acting parts and a group director. "Students identify difficult turns of phrase or specific vocabulary words and make their best educated guess as to meaning. They run lines with one another to improve pronunciation and dramatic reading. The director makes suggestions as to simple stage movements that can be done in the small space at the front of the room. The group discusses appropriate tone, body language, and facial expression. Concerning themselves with the dramatic aspects of presenting to the other three groups more or less forces them to make meaning. Each group takes a turn in a kind of 'drama slam.' They try to outdo the others and get delightfully hammy."

Demonstrating Understanding of Terms

I find that asking students to create something to show that they understand a word, whether it is a picture, a rap, a video, or a commercial, is always beneficial. To present the information creatively, they must understand the concept at a deeper level, and giving students choices always increases their ownership in the project.

I talked with a teacher who uses poetry to teach content-area vocabulary. Before the test, her students work in small groups to create poems about the vocabulary words. She uses haiku, the Japanese patterned three-line poem. The first line must include five syllables, the second line must contain seven syllables, and third line must contain five syllables. It challenges to students to condense the information and present it following the pattern.

Haiku About the Atmosphere

Atmosphere, it's here
Around the Earth in layers
N, O, H, and more

Just after that conversation, I read an article in the *New York Times* about a blogger who encourages the use of the Fibonacci sequence to write six-line poems. What an interesting idea for explaining math terms!

Fibonacci Sequence Poem About Divisibility

1 Math
1 House
2 Divide
3 Whole numbers
5 Remainder zero
8 When the last digit is even
5 Then divide by 2
3 The answer
2 Should be
1 A
1 Whole

Amber, Grade 7

Procedures When Encountering New Vocabulary

My students initially struggled with my desire for them to understand vocabulary on their own. Their first response—in fact, their only strategy for figuring out the new word—was to ask the teacher. I'm sure that at some time in an earlier grade level, they had learned other strategies, but they didn't use them, and they no longer recognized there were other strategies. I decided to capitalize on what worked in my classroom. I had a set of rules for discipline that they understood and respected; why not try the same thing for vocabulary? So I developed a set of procedures for what to do when they didn't know a new word. They quickly learned to try other options before they came to me. One of the things I did was make the alternative strategies visible and understandable.

Over time, I've adapted the procedures as I've worked with other teachers, but the premise remains the same. Teach or remind students of effective strategies, keep them visible to everyone, and teach students to be independent. If your students keep a journal, have them designate a section and keep a log of strategies that have worked for them in the past. For example, if drawing a picture helps them remember a key concept, write that down so that they will remember it next time.

What to Do When You Don't Know a Vocabulary Word

- Try to figure it out on your own.
- Read the sentence to understand the meaning.
- Look for prefixes or suffixes that you know to help you understand the word.
- Check to see whether the word is in the glossary or margin of the book.
- Look it up in the dictionary.
- Use a thesaurus.
- Ask three other students for help.
- If nothing else works, ask the teacher.

For many students, encountering new words creates fear and confusion. But if you use these simple techniques, you can help them unlock the mysteries of language.

Summary

- Memorizing does not equal learning. True mastery of a word goes far beyond the ability to copy a definition and recognize it on a test.
- Students need multiple exposures to new terminology. Provide a variety of opportunities for students to encounter each word.
- Using visuals may increase student understanding. Literally show them what a word means.
- Make learning vocabulary fun by incorporating games and hands-on activities.
- Teach your students how to unlock the meaning of an unknown word so that they will be able to acquire meaning on their own in the future.

If You Would Like More Information…

This site provides teachers with multiple instruction strategies to teaching vocabulary. http://www.webenglishteacher.com/vocab.html

Bringing Words to Life: Robust Vocabulary Instruction by I. Beck, M. McKeown, & L. Kucan, The Guilford Press.

Integrated Vocabulary Instruction: Meeting the Needs of Diverse Learners in Grades K-5 by Blachowicz, Fisher, & Watts-Taffe, Learning Points Associates.

Vocabulary Connections by Jill Norris, Incentive Publications.

The Vocabulary-Enriched Classroom: Practices for Improving the Reading Performance of All Students in Grades 3 and Up by Cathy Block and John Mangiere, Scholastic.

W

Working Together Makes a Difference

When you first assemble a group, it's not a team right off the bat. It's only a collection of individuals.

Coach Mike Krzyzewski

Think About It

Do your students work in groups, or do they just sit together?

Group work is one of the most effective ways to help students learn. It can increase student motivation and is an important life skill. When I was teaching, some of my students didn't like to work in groups. They complained every day until I brought in a newspaper article that said the number one reason people were fired from their jobs was that they couldn't get along with their coworkers. That was an eye-opener for my students.

Recently, I was talking with a project manager, and I asked him about the importance of teamwork. He pointed out that knowing how to work with other people is critical. "The more successful you are, the more important it is to influence, motivate, and work with others. If you think about successful people, working with people becomes your job; that is what you do."

That's pretty insightful. For people who have achieved high levels of success in the workplace, no matter what the setting, teamwork isn't part of their job, *it is their job.* As a teacher, this reminds me that if I believe I should prepare my students for life after school, then I need to teach them to work together.

Recently, I was in a classroom in which the teacher bragged to me that her students worked in groups all the time. When I asked her students, they told me that the desks are placed in groups, but they just read the book silently and answer questions individually. After thinking for a minute, one student said, "We can ask each other for help if we need to." That's not really group work. Effective group activities provide opportunities for your students to work together, either with a partner, a small group, or the entire class, to accomplish a task. In these instances, everyone has a specific role, and there are clear individual and shared responsibilities. Missy Miles uses a rubric (see page 136) for assessing each GROUP in her classroom.

Structures for Effective Group Work

First, determine how you want to organize your groups. Do you want students to work in pairs, groups of four, or some other organization? Will your students stay in the same group for a long period of time? I find that balance is important. For example, students need to learn to work together over time. Shannon Knowles explains that in a setting such as a science lab, "I try not to change groups. My kids realized if they complained about other group members, I'd change the groups, so now I explain as they get older, in the real world, you have to work with someone you don't like, so I don't change as often now."

However, I also think students should work with a variety of people, and they should not be limited to working with the same students all the time. In my classroom, I used groups of four for some activities and pairs for other activities. I switched my students around often enough that they rarely complained about other group members. They knew that I expected them to learn to work with everyone and that they would be grouped with someone else later.

Cooperative Learning Rubric

	You're a Team Player!	You're Working on It…	You're Flying Solo
G Group dedication	The student is totally dedicated to his or her group, offering all of his or her attention by actively listening to peers and responding with ideas.	The student is partially dedicated to his or her group though sometimes becomes distracted by students or issues outside the group.	The student spends most of his or her time focusing on things outside the group; he or she is not available for discussion or group work.
R Responsibility	The student shares responsibility equally with other group members and accepts his or her role in the group.	The student takes on responsibility but does not completely fulfill his or her obligations.	The student either tries to take over the group and does not share responsibilities or takes no part at all in the group work assigned.
O Open communication	The student gives polite and constructive criticism to group members when necessary, welcomes feedback from peers, resolves conflict peacefully, and asks questions when a group goal is unclear.	The student gives criticism, though often in a blunt manner, reluctantly accepts criticism from peers, and may not resolve conflict peacefully all of the time.	The student is quick to point out the faults of other group members yet is unwilling to take any criticism in return; often, the students argues with peers rather than calmly coming to a consensus.
U Utilization of work time	The student is always on task, working with group members to achieve goals, objectives, and deadlines.	The student is on task most of the time but occasionally takes time off from working with the group.	The student does not pay attention to the task at hand and frustrates other group members because of his or her inability to complete work in a timely fashion.
P Participation	The student is observed sharing ideas, reporting research findings to the group, taking notes from other members, and offering assistance to his or her peers as needed.	The student sometimes shares ideas or reports findings openly but rarely takes notes from other group members.	This student does not openly share ideas or findings with the group, nor does he or she take notes on peers'

Selection of Group Members

Next, decide how the groups will be formed. Will students be allowed to choose their groups? In my classroom, I allowed students to self-select their groups on rare occasions. Most of the time, I assigned groups in order to manage bullying and negative peer influences. This is up to you, as you know your students. There are times you will want to assign groups based on skill levels or interests; just be sure you don't label students by always assigning them to certain groups.

Barbara Liebhaber uses a variety of methods to randomly assign students to groups. "Besides the usual color- or number-coded pieces of paper or counting off, I shuffle playing cards and each student takes one. While they are taking their cards, I make up the rules. Find your group by matching either the suit, the number, or picture. I prepare the deck ahead of time so that I have the correct number of cards that will create the desired number of groups."

Roles for Group Members

A critical step is structuring your group activity. Create an activity that requires each student to contribute to the task. It's important to assign roles for your students, although you may want students within a group to choose their roles. The roles may change depending on your assignment. For example, if students are working on a lab experiment, you will need a safety monitor and a materials manager. However, if your project is developing a Web page, you might prefer a webmaster and a layout editor.

Sample Roles and Responsibilities

Facilitator—Leader of the group; facilitates action
Recorder—Records comments and/or work
Reporter—Reports work to the entire group
Materials manager—Collects and distributes materials
Time keeper—Keeps the group working within time limits
Wildcard—Assistant to the leader; fills in holes
Encourager—Encourages others
Summarizer—Summarizes work and may report to the class
Fact checker—Checks work from group; researches facts
Reflector—reflects on comments from group, asks probing questions
Designer—Designs the project
Creator—Creates or builds the design

I encourage you to rotate the roles within the team for different assignments so that one or two students do not dominate the group activities. You should also take time to teach students about their roles and responsibilities. As Duke University basketball coach Mike Krzyzewski reminds us, it takes time and intentionality to transform a set of individuals into an effective team.

Rules

In addition to your standard classroom rules, you may need a couple of simple rules that are specific to group activities. I found that I needed to discuss my expectations for the noise level of the classroom. For example, I wanted my students to talk to each other. But they needed to talk to their group members, not the entire class. You might come up with a catchy way to describe an appropriate noise level, such as "Bees Buzz." Bees buzz when they are being productive (making honey), but they don't shout. I was in another classroom in which the teacher talked about using your "12-inch voice." Her students knew that meant that people within a foot (within the group) should be able hear you, but not those outside the group (more than a foot away).

I also used a rule called "ask three before me." This one works when your students are in groups of four. It simply means that a student should ask his or her group members for help before asking the teacher. This encourages students to look to each other for support instead of always looking to the teacher first. It's up to you to decide what rules you need in your classroom. Be sure that your students understand your expectations, and monitor the groups continuously to ensure that all students have an opportunity to participate.

Effective Groups in Action

Erin Owens applies these concepts with her first graders. "When working in teams, my students each have a job or responsibility. They work really hard because they want to be an active member of the team and participate in the group's discussion or project. Also, they want their friends to know how creative and smart they can be. Every child is capable of experiencing success in groups. Their responsibility usually incorporates their strengths. As an example, I have had poor readers who are detailed, skilled artists; so, they illustrate. Every child is perceived as talented in my room. Most of all they are enjoying the process of learning; it is meaningful and social. They enjoy gaining ideas from friends as much as they enjoy sharing them. It is amazing what groups of children can accomplish."

Michael Ritch's middle school students apply what they learn about weather and the atmosphere through group research projects. Group members choose a weather event such as a blizzard or flood. Using a clear rubric as a guide, they create a scenario for that event. Members of the group complete different portions of the project, ranging from writing a script, filming the news footage, building the set, or acting, either as the meteorologist on the scene or the studio reporter.

As Michael describes, "In the end, they have a weather movie that looks like they are working for the Weather Channel reporting on a hurricane or tornado. We have a day where we premiere all the movies. Parents, administrators, and other teachers attend to watch the movies on a big screen in the media center or on the wall in my room. At the end, they fill out surveys talking about what they learned about weather, acting, writing, and how well they thought their group worked. Each student is held accountable for his or her part in the project. In the past, students have designed pulley systems to dump ice on people in a hail storm, or they have stood underneath the shower in my room to act like they are in a heavy rainfall. The creativity of the students to make it look real is really something. One of the best things is that they are teaching one another about how weather forms and how to stay safe."

These group projects were effective because the teachers created meaningful activities, designed structures that ensured individual and group success, provided instruction to support the process, and made learning fun. And their students responded in a positive way!

Summary

- Learning to work effectively with those around you is a life skill. As teachers, we must help students become successful and productive in group settings.
- The structure of the group and the selection of members are crucial. Make conscious decisions about the arrangement that maximizes the potential for success in each group.
- When each member of the group is a contributor, teamwork is achieved. To accomplish this, assign specific roles or tasks for each student.
- Establish clear rules and expectations for group work from the beginning to ensure time on task and productivity.
- Teach students how to work together and monitor their progress. Group work is a skill that requires practice.

If You Would Like More Information…

This site is about cooperative learning: http://edtech.kennesaw.edu/intech/cooperativelearning.html/.

Cooperative Learning: Theory, Research, and Practice (2nd Edition) by Robert E. Slavin, Allyn & Bacon.

The Teacher's Sourcebook for Cooperative Learning by G. Jacobs, Corwin Press.

X

X Factor

Your heart is slightly bigger than the average human heart, but that's because you're a teacher.

Aaron Bacall

In my graduate classes, we read a variety of research studies about schools and learning. In most of the reports, the authors point out the power of a teacher. As teachers, we know this—we have tremendous power. We can inspire, we can support, and we can help our students rise to levels they can only imagine.

You set the tone in your classroom. If you want to be there, your students will also want to be in class. If you are upset, they know that and they will respond, sometimes in less than positive ways. If you think that Barney can't answer a question, he'll believe you. Or if you know that Sh'Quandra can complete a science project for the science fair, she'll prove you right. Because of the influence that we have on our students, it's important for us to make choices that will help us maximize our influence in positive ways.

Make a CHOICE

C	Clarify your vision
H	Hold high expectations
O	Operate from a students-first perspective
I	Inspire your students through a positive environment
C	Count the positives
E	Encourage and motivate yourself

Clarify Your Vision

The first and most important step that you can take to set the tone in your classroom is to clarify your vision. Who are you as a teacher? What do you believe? Where do you want your students to be when they leave you? Make a list, draw a sketch, or write a letter with the answers to those questions. Then use your vision to drive your actions throughout the year. If you want your students to be problem solvers, give them problems to solve, not just simple questions to answer. If you want your students to see you as an advocate for their learning, then care and learn about who they are so that you can truly be their advocate. On any given day, you'll face a multitude of options for how to spend your time and how to set your priorities. Having a clear vision will help you make choices that are most likely to help you and your students arrive at your desired destination.

Think About It

Who are you as a teacher? What do you believe? Where do you want your students to be when they leave you?

Hold High Expectations

How high are your expectations for yourself and your students? Often, I talk to teachers who are feel tired and discouraged by the outside forces that affect education. Education is the only career in which almost everyone else thinks they can tell you how to do your job. Because each person has been a student, some think that qualifies them to tell you what to do. Increasing pressure to measure teachers by nothing more than test scores can cause you to wonder whether you should just give up and follow a script for your students.

Don't! You are too important, and so are your students. Follow your standards, pay attention to the expectations of accountability and testing, but don't be limited by them. Dream big dreams. Imagine what can happen this year if you and your students work together to grow and learn. Be creative. Take risks for your students. As I visit classrooms, I meet teachers who dare to move beyond the requirements of teaching to the artistry. Be one of those teachers.

Operate from a Students-First Perspective

On my office refrigerator, I have a sign that asks, "How would ____________ positively impact student learning?" A principal gave it to me when I explained that most high-performing schools make decisions based on the answer to that question. After I shared the question with my graduate students, several of them told me that it completely changed how they think about what happens in their schools. Operating from a students-first perspective means that we filter our instructional choices through this question, choosing the answer that has the most positive impact on student learning.

How Would?

- How would incorporating visuals into my classroom positively affect student learning?
- How would holding my students to a "Not Yet" grading policy positively affect student learning?
- How would increasing lab activities and decreasing worksheets positively affect student learning?
- How would providing students opportunities to take responsibility for their own learning positively affect student learning?

Inspire Your Students Through a Positive Environment

Our environment has an influence on us. I recently visited a school where the walls were barren and trash filled the floors. Even though it was a newer building, the morale was low, and that was reflected in the environment. Students didn't seem to care about school, and teachers seemed to struggle to speak. On the other hand, I also visited an older building where everyone had a smile for me. The walls were plastered with samples of students' work and inspiring quotes that reflected the positive morale of the school. My first teaching job was at Marion Elementary School. The principal divided the walls of the older building into small sections. Each student painted one section to decorate the building. I still remember walking into the building for the first time and realizing that students were the focus. Make your classroom an inviting place, and you and your students will learn more.

Count the Positives

Every day, I make a list of the positive things that happened. I've found that if I don't, I tend to forget that there were any positives. If your days are typical, you deal with a good number of negative events. There are negative comments, lessons that didn't work as well as you'd anticipated, or complaints about something you did. The list is endless, and we tend to remember the negatives. Writing a list at the end of each day or each class not only helps you remember the positive things that happened but also forces you to look for the good in any situation. When my graduate students come into class, our first activity is to share something good about their students. They've learned that even if they had a bad week, they can find lots of good things that happened. And on days that are particularly tough, when you are struggling to find light in the darkness, you can revisit your list to help you remember that you do make a difference.

Encourage and Motivate Yourself

That leads us to the final point: You need to continually motivate yourself. If you don't encourage yourself, you won't be able to encourage your students. Often, we spend so much time helping others that we forget to take time for ourselves. Take five minutes every day for yourself, and use that time to remind yourself of your power as a teacher. Sam Myers, coordinator of the alternative school in Sumter 17 School District, says, "On your worst day, you are someone's best hope." Your students need you. Take care of yourself.

Encouraging Yourself

- Build a positive memory file of notes.
- Read books that inspire you.
- Watch inspirational movies.
- Find everyday heroes.
- Surround yourself with motivating thoughts.
- Keep a success journal.

Summary

- You have power! You are the most important factor in the success of your classroom—success that goes beyond school.
- The choices that you make each day have profound impact on the students you teach.
- Set a clear vision for your classroom to remind yourself of your values.
- Embrace the art of teaching; don't settle for merely meeting testing requirements.
- Your students come first. Always imagine how they will view the things you do and say.
- Remain positive in your actions and words to inspire students to greatness.
- You can't encourage others if you don't feel encouragement yourself. Find your source of motivation and tap into it daily.

If You Would Like More Information...

The Teacher's Reflective Calendar and Planning Journal: Motivation, Inspiration, and Affirmation by Mary McGrath and Beverley Johns, Corwin Press.

The Inviting School Treasury: 1024 Ways to Invite Student Success in Your School by William Purkey and Paula Stanley, Scholastic Trade.

Y

Yawn! Reading Aloud Is Boring

It's such a wonderful feeling to watch a child discover that reading is a marvelous adventure rather than a chore.

Zilpha Keatley Snyder

As I visit classrooms, one of the most common activities I see is students reading aloud in class. Despite its familiarity, reading aloud is also one of the most ineffective methods of instruction. Just because we do something a lot doesn't mean it works.

Think About It

Does the poem describe your experience with reading aloud in your classroom?

Round-Robin Reading

Round-robin reading, straight down the row
One person's reading with the rest of us in tow
I am seated second, so I'm practicing my section
The last kid on the row's got several paragraphs of protection
He doesn't need to listen till the person before him reads
And so he's off in his own world until he finally heeds
The teacher's warning to follow along—he fakes it for a minute
No one's paying attention at all to the story or what's in it
Only one attends to the task at hand—the one who has her turn
But once her turn is finished, she soon will cease to learn
The other rows are sleeping or engaged in untimely deeds
It's seems obvious to us that during "reading" no one reads
Doesn't the teacher get it? This activity is a waste
I guess she doesn't notice, coz she's pacing the room in haste
"Follow along, pay attention
Pick your heads up or you'll go to detention!
Don't hit, don't throw, don't move, don't sleep
Don't tease, don't draw, don't make a peep!"
Open your eyes, please, teacher, round robin is torture for us
One student reads a paragraph while the rest of us get fussed
There has to be a better way to give us what we need
A way that would be interesting—a way where we'd actually READ!

Annette Breaux

The most traditional form of reading aloud is round robin reading. You probably experienced this as a student; I certainly did. Everyone was assigned a short section to read, and we took turns reading our part from the story or textbook. The first problem with this method is that each student is reading ahead to his or her section rather than listening to the student who is currently reading. As Annette Breaux points out in her poem, rather than paying attention, I'm preparing for my turn.

Recently, several teachers told me they have solved that problem by shifting to "popcorn reading." They randomly call on students to read so that students can't read ahead. Although that addresses one problem, it doesn't solve the major issue with reading aloud: The method requires students to perform without practicing.

Performing Without Practicing

Let me give you a personal example that I experienced recently. I was planning to sing "Happy Birthday" to a very good friend of mine. Now, although I am a self-confident adult, I know my limitations. I'm not a great singer, and my friend is. So I was nervous. I practiced for two weeks, and I still needed reassurance and coaching from another friend before my "performance." Then, as I prepared to sing, my stomach was filled with butterflies.

If you like to sing, you're probably laughing at me right now. After all, it isn't a hard song—it's just "Happy Birthday." But I have high standards for myself, and I don't like to stumble in front of other people. And because I'm successful in some areas, such as speaking to large groups, I stress when I think that I may not be successful.

Doesn't that sound exactly like some of your students? And I'm not talking about just your at-risk readers. Often, your high achievers who are perfectionists struggle with this issue. When I'm put on the spot and asked to stand up and perform something, you simply aren't going to get my best work. And the stress of the situation outweighs most of the benefits. During oral reading, the focus on performance can undermine a student's reading and fluency skills.

Only a few of your most confident readers will thrive in this environment. Even if you tell me that your students like to read out loud without any chance to prepare, the activity still involves only one student at a time. Why settle for instruction that does not engage all of your students?

Other Options

Let's look at two alternatives that can involve all of your students and lead to deeper understanding of the content. In paired reading, two partners read the selection together. Your instructions should include students' use of soft voices because multiple sets of partners will be reading together at the same time. I heard one teacher say, "Use your six-inch voices," which meant that their voices should not be heard six inches away from their partner. You can also have small groups read silently, then practice together so that they can read aloud to the whole group. Both of these methods will allow all of your students to work together to read and understand.

> **Think About It**
>
> How can you incorporate partner and/or small-group reading in your classroom?

Interactive Reading Guides

A more structured approach is the use of an interactive reading guide. As you can see in the sample, students work together in pairs to read a section of text. This method is equally effective with fiction or nonfiction. As a teacher, you build structure into the lesson through the guide. I like this method because it allows me to break the content into smaller chunks for my students. I can mix silent reading, reading together, and single read-alouds together to best meet the needs of my students.

Social Studies Interactive Reading Guide

Chapter 5, Lesson 3 (pages 99–115)

Individually:	Survey this lesson by skimming the headings, maps, and captions.
Together:	Discuss the information that you expect to find in this lesson. Create an outline of the information.
Individually:	Read the "Think About What You Know" question at the top of page 99. Answer this question in two to three sentences on your paper.
Together:	Share your answers.
Partner A:	Read Section A, "Spaniards Search for the Seven Cities of Gold."
Partner B:	Read Section B, "Exploring the American Southwest." Read your section silently to prepare for the next two steps.
Partner A:	Orally, read Section A, "Spaniards Search for the Seven Cities of Gold." Remember that you are reading only to your partner, not to the entire class.
Together:	Summarize the section in five to six sentences and record your summary in your notes. Underline the names of important people and places in your summary.
Partner B:	Orally, read Section B, "Exploring the American Southwest." Remember that you are reading only to your partner, not to the entire class.
Individually:	Answer Question B under the Lesson 3 review on page 149.
Together:	Discuss your answers and make sure you agree. If not, go back to the text to decide who is correct.
Together:	Discuss the following question: Why do you think the Indians repeatedly told Coronado and other Spanish explorers about wealthy cities that did not exist? Record your answer.

Individually:	Using the map on page 146, label your own maps and draw each explorer's route. Use a different color for each explorer.
Together:	Compare your maps. Are there any differences?
Together:	Record all of the Spanish explorers' names from Chapter 5, what they explored, and what they found. Use the chart on page 115.

Explorer	Explored	Found

Ensuring Understanding During Silent Reading

Tracy Smith, a former English teacher, prefers to have all of her students read independently. But she also ensures that her students understand what they are reading through the use of bookmarks. As she explains, "Students read books of their choice, and prepare bookmarks about their books. The bookmarks might include their questions, predictions, observations about the author's purpose or craft, reflections on the characters, or other personal connections. Each day, during our reading time, I circulate and talk to students about their books, including their reasons for choosing particular books and authors. This promotes an open discussion about literacy in our classroom. Often students recommend their books to me and to each other. Isn't this our goal with reading instruction—to develop real readers?"

Choosing Oral Reading

Ultimately, you may choose to incorporate oral reading in your classroom. And reading aloud can be more engaging if you incorporate four simple principles.

Principals for ORAL Reading

O	Ownership from students
R	Relevant activity
A	Allow practice prior to performing
L	Listening with interest for a purpose

Involve your students in decisions about making oral reading more effective. Ask for their input. They may suggest acting out a story or demonstrating their understanding of the content by reading it as if they were performing on television, all of which are more exciting than traditional read-aloud lessons. These examples are also more relevant because they create opportunities for reading aloud that simulate real-life experiences. Remember to allow students to practice first. The additional time that you invest will pay off in higher levels of learning. Finally, be sure that all of your students have a purpose for listening. It can also heighten interest if they are listening to new material. By making these simple adjustments, your students will be more successful, and, as Zilpha Keatley Snyder points out, your students will be less likely to view reading as a chore.

Summary

- Reading aloud as a form of whole-group instruction does not involve the whole group; it only involves one person at a time.
- During round-robin reading, students do not comprehend the text. Instead, each student is focused on pronouncing the words in their section of the text.
- Try out alternatives to round-robin or popcorn reading to get each student involved.
- Allow rehearsal time. Anyone can appreciate the opportunity to practice before the game; this applies to readers, too!
- Comprehension will deepen if readers are provided opportunities to interact with the text at their own pace. Teacher-created reading guides help students get the most out of a selection of text.
- When reading aloud in class, allow opportunities for student input, provide relevant text, give a purpose, and let students practice.

If You Would Like More Information…

This site lists alternatives to round robin reading. http://classroom.jc-schools.net/read/RoundRobinReading.pdf#search=%22%2Bbook%2C%20%2B%22round%20robin%20reading%22%22

Round Robin Reading: Considering Alternative Instructional Practices that Make More Sense by Patricia Kelly, Reading Horizons, 36(2).

The Round Robin Reading Debate by Susan Mandel Glaser. Teaching PreK-8, October, 2006.

Good-bye Round Robin: 25 Effective Oral Reading Strategies by Michael Opitz and Timothy Rasinski, Heinemann.

Z

Zoom In and Zoom Out

If you have built castles in the air, your work need not be lost; that is where they should be. Now put the foundations under them!

Henry David Thoreau

Finally, it's important to remember that all of our instruction should balance the big picture with smaller details. I was recently in Buffalo, New York, on a business trip with a colleague. A friend of ours from graduate school picked us up at the airport. Because he was familiar with the area, we didn't print out directions to the hotel. I was in the back seat, listening to a basketball game, when they asked me the location of the hotel. After they handed me a map, I glanced at the reservation, saw the hotel was on Maple, pointed out Maple on the map, and went back to listening to the game. An hour later, I realized we were still driving. The hotel was on Maple Drive, but I had found Maple Street on the map because I wasn't paying attention to the details. It's a good thing my colleagues knew me—they joked that they should never have asked me a question during a ball game! I was focused on the big picture when I needed to zoom in on the details.

My students tended to focus on one or the other, but they were less able to balance broad concepts and details. For example, sometimes all they wanted to do was memorize isolated facts in case they needed to know the information for a test. That was important, but they would focus on the details so much that they forgot to connect it with other information they knew.

Zooming In

There are creative ways to ask students to focus on specific details. First, make sure they understand why the details are important. Though there are times when we don't need to memorize the minutia of every concept, there are times when we need to pay attention to each particular part of a task. After all, if you are cooking, you don't want to skip a step. One time, I asked my students to write out a set of simple directions for making a peanut butter and jelly sandwich. Then, their partner had to follow the directions, exactly as written. They realized the importance of being specific when they discovered that they had forgotten an important step, such as opening the jar of peanut butter.

Charlesetta Dawson applies this concept in her integrated arts class. Her students design a map of a dance. "They must create symbols and draw a key of the symbols to represent the types of moves, such as a slide, hop, skip, spin, turn, or whatever. The dance must start at one part (north, south, east, or west), and, to complete the dance, you must travel all different directions. Students typically color code the map." Students swap maps and have to follow the dance. Finally, they discuss the changes that are needed to complete the dance as designed by the first student.

Zooming Out

Some students excel at connecting learning to what they already know and to their lives; other students struggle with it. At the end of every class discussion or every reading, my students know what I'm going to ask: "How does this relate to other items we have discussed?" or "How does this apply to you?" I believe it's critical for students to make those connections every time we learn something new rather than wait until there is so much information that they are overwhelmed. You can do this orally by asking students to turn to a partner and share their responses or through written exit slips.

Zooming In and Zooming Out

Throughout your instruction, build ways to help your students see both views. You can use a two-column chart on which students write down the big ideas from your lesson or from the text in the left column and the details within each idea in the right column. Or, you might ask students to use sticky notes during reading: one color to signify the broad concepts and a second color to highlight important facts.

Kendra Alston uses a zoom in and zoom out strategy whenever she introduces a new concept to her students. She starts by writing the topic on the board. Then she asks each student to brainstorm whatever comes to mind about the topic in the small box. She finds this less threatening to students than asking them to fill out an entire sheet of paper. Next, they share those answers with a partner. She then gives students a short article to read and has them fill out the class notes section. When they are finished, they again share with a partner.

After they have discussed what they read, she guides a class discussion of the material, first "zooming in" on the most and least important things they learned, as well as something they didn't expect to learn. Throughout the discussion, she writes individual answers on the board. The class then rates the answers, and students can choose which answers they want to add to their personal notes. She purposely doesn't rush the process, allowing students plenty of time to become familiar with the text, absorb what they are learning and share with others.

Next, she "zooms out," asking students to take what they have learned and compare it to something else that it is similar and write down other related ideas. This requires students to take the small, isolated learning of the day and place it in the broad landscape of their knowledge and lives.

Students performing at the highest levels of learning understand this simple concept. There is a time for the landscape view, and there is a time to pay attention to small details. Understanding is a tool, and you need to use the right tool. Sometimes you need binoculars; other times you need a magnifying glass.

Zooming In and Zooming Out

Topic:

Brainstorming notes:

Class notes from reading:

Zoom In

Most important: ______________________________

____

Least important: ______________________________

____

Would not expect: ______________________________

____

Zoom Out

Similar to: ______________________________

____

Related ideas: ______________________________

____

Summary Statement

____

____

____

____

____

____

____

Summary

- Teach students when it is necessary to focus on the details and when it is important to step back and look at the big picture.
- Find creative ways to teach your students how to zoom in on the specifics during a lesson.
- Some students need to be guided through the process of making connections; it is a skill that should be included in your instructional plans.
- To maximize learning, take time at the end of each lesson to help students zoom in and zoom out.

If You Would Like More Information…

This site is an A to Z teacher resource that provides resources for different themes: http://www.atozteacherstuff.com/

This site provides lesson plans that encourage students to make connections: http://mconn.doe.state.la.us/lessonplans.php

This site provides a lesson plan for reading comprehension that encourages students to make connections with what they are learning: http://www.readwritethink.org/lessons/lesson_view.asp?id=228

Bibliography

ACT. (2006). *Reading between the lines: What the ACT reveals about college readiness in reading.* Iowa City, IA: ACT. Retrieved October 17, 2006, from http://www.act.org/path/policy/pdf/readingreport.pdf.

Allen, J. (2004). *Tools for teaching content literacy.* Portland, ME: Stenhouse.

Allen, J. (2004). *Yellow brick roads: Shared and guided paths to independent reading 4–12.* Portland, ME: Stenhouse.

Alvarado, A., & Herr, P. (2003). *Inquiry-based learning using everyday objects: Hands-on instructional strategies that promote active learning in grades 3–8.* Thousand Oaks, CA: Corwin Press.

Baldwin, M. D., Keating, J. F., & Bachman, K. J. (2006). *Teaching in secondary schools: Meeting the challenges of today's adolescent.* Upper Saddle River, NJ: Pearson/Merrill/Prentice Hall.

Blackburn, B. R. (2005). *Classroom motivation from A to Z: How to engage your students in learning.* Larchmont, NY: Eye On Education.

Blackburn, B. R., & Norton, T. (2004, Spring). Content area literacy: One district's efforts to integrate reading and writing across the curriculum. *South Carolina Middle School Association Journal,* 13–15.

Breaux, A. L. (2003). *101 "answers" for new teachers and their mentors: Effective teaching tips for daily classroom use.* Larchmont, NY: Eye On Education.

Bridgeland, J. M, DiIulio, J. J., & Morison, K. B. (2006). *The silent epidemic: Perspectives of high school dropouts.* Seattle, WA: Bill and Melinda Gates Foundation. Retrieved October 17, 2006, from http://www.gatesfoundation.org/nr/downloads/ed/thesilentepidemic3-06final.pdf.

Callahan, J. F., Clark, L. H., & Kellough, R. D. (1998). *Teaching in the middle and secondary schools* (6th ed.). Upper Saddle River, NJ: Merrill.

Chapman, C., & King, R. (2005). *Differentiated assessment strategies: One tool doesn't fit all.* Thousand Oaks, CA: Corwin Press.

Cole, A. D. (2002). *Better answers: Written performance that looks good and sounds smart.* Portland, ME: Stenhouse.

Cunningham, P. M., & Allington, R. L (1999). *Classrooms that work: They can all read and write* (2nd ed.). New York: Longman.

Erwin, J. C. (2004). *The classroom of choice: Giving students what they need and getting what you want.* Alexandria, VA: Association for Supervision and Curriculum Development.

Fiedling, L., & Roller, C. (1992, May). Making difficult books accessible and easy books acceptable. *The Reading Teacher,* 678–685.

Frank, T. H. (2005). *The handbook for developing supportive learning environments.* Larchmont, NY: Eye On Education.

Gaskins, I. W. (2005). *Success with struggling readers: The Benchmark School approach.* New York: Guilford Press.

Graves, M. F., & Graves, B. B. (2003). *Scaffolding reading experiences: Designs for student success* (2nd ed.). Norwood, MA: Christopher-Gordon.

Harmin, M. (1994). *Inspiring active learning: A handbook for teachers.* Alexandria, VA: Association for Supervision and Curriculum Development.

Howard, D. L., Fogarty, R., & Pete, B. (2004). *Teaching and learning: An anthology for professional teachers.* Chicago: Robin Fogarty & Associates.

Jacobs, G. M., Power, M. A., & Inn, L. W. (2002). *The teacher's sourcebook for cooperative learning: Practical techniques, basic principles, and frequently asked questions.* Thousand Oaks, CA: Corwin Press.

Kellough, R. D., & Carjuzaa, J. (2006). *Teaching in the middle and secondary schools* (8th ed.). Upper Saddle River, NJ: Pearson/Merrill/Prentice Hall.

Marchand-Martella, N. E., Slocum, T. A., & Martella, R. C. (2004). *Introduction to direct instruction.* Boston: Pearson.

Martinello, M. L., & Cook, G. E. (2000). *Interdisciplinary inquiry in teaching and learning* (2nd ed.). Upper Saddle River, NJ: Merrill.

Marzano, R. J. (2004). *Building background knowledge for academic achievement: Research on what works in schools.* Alexandria, VA: Association for Supervision and Curriculum Development.

Marzano, R. J., & Pickering, D. J. (2005). *Building academic vocabulary: Teacher's manual.* Alexandria, VA: Association for Supervision and Curriculum Development.

Marzano, R. J., Pickering, D. J., & Pollock, J. E. (2001). *Classroom instruction that works: research-based strategies for increasing student achievement.* Alexandria, VA: Association for Supervision and Curriculum Development.

McKenna, M. C., & Robinson, R. D. (2005). *Teaching through text: Reading and writing in the content areas* (4th ed.). Boston: Allyn and Bacon.

Raphael, T. (1986). Teaching question-and-answer relationships, revisited. *The Reading Teacher, 39*(6), 516–522.

Santa, C., Havens, L., & Macumber, E. (1996). *Creating independence through student-owned strategies.* Dubuque, IA: Kendall/Hunt.

Schlechty, P. C. (2002). *Working on the work: An action plan for teachers, principals, and superintendents.* San Francisco: Jossey-Bass.

Silver, D. (2005). *Drumming to the beat of different marchers: Finding the rhythm for differentiated learning.* Nashville, TN: Incentive Publications.

Simkins, M., Cole, K., Tavalin, F., & Means, B. (2002). *Increasing student learning through multimedia projects.* Alexandria, VA: Association for Supervision and Curriculum Development.

Southern Regional Education Board (SREB). (2004). *Literacy across the curriculum: Setting and implementing goals for grades six through 12* (Site Development Guide No. 12). Atlanta, GA: Author.

Sprenger, M. (2005). *How to teach so students remember.* Alexandria, VA: Association for Supervision and Curriculum Development.

Strong, R. W., Silver, H. F., & Perini, M. J. (2001). *Teaching what matters most: Standards and strategies for raising student achievement.* Alexandria, VA: Association for Supervision and Curriculum Development.

Tomlinson, C. A. (1999). *The differentiated classroom: Responding to the needs of all learners.* Alexandria, VA: Association for Supervision and Curriculum Development.

Tomlinson, C. A., & Eidson, C. C. (2003). *Differentiation in practice: A resource guide for differentiating curriculum, grades 5–9.* Alexandria, VA: Association for Supervision and Curriculum Development.

Wiederhold, C. (1995). *Cooperative Learning and Higher Level Thinking: The Q-Matrix.* San Clemente, CA: Kagan Publishing.

Wiggins, G. P. (1993). *Assessing student performance: Exploring the purpose and limits of testing.* San Francisco: Jossey-Bass.

Wormeli, R. (2005). *Summarization in any subject: 50 techniques to improve student learning.* Alexandria, VA: Association for Supervision and Curriculum Development.

Wormeli, R. (2006). *Fair isn't always equal: Assessing and grading in the differentiated classroom.* Portland, ME: Stenhouse.

Worthy, J., Broaddus, K., & Ivey, G. (2001). *Pathways to independence: Reading, writing, and learning in grades 3–8.* New York: Guilford Press.